AF480625

Raised by Ghosts

Between Three Graves

A Daughter's Story of Loss,
Survival and Forgiveness

Karlin Kilburn

This is a work of nonfiction. Some names and identifying details have been changed to protect the privacy of individuals. Other names are used with permission.

First Edition

ISBN: 979-8-9954776-1-7

Cover design by Karlin Kilburn

Printed in the United States of America

Quiet Grace

PUBLISHING

Dedication

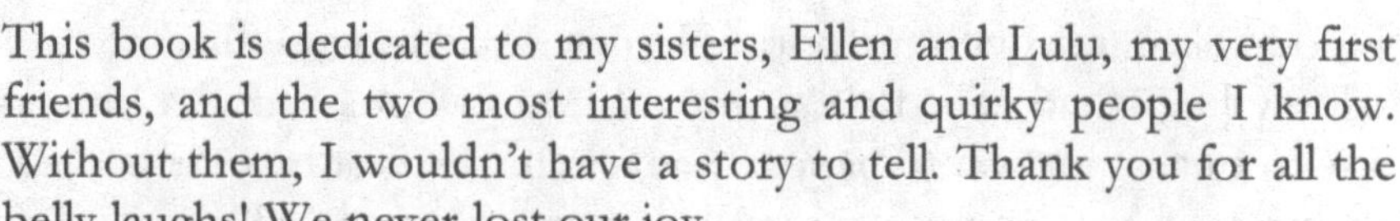

This book is dedicated to my sisters, Ellen and Lulu, my very first friends, and the two most interesting and quirky people I know. Without them, I wouldn't have a story to tell. Thank you for all the belly laughs! We never lost our joy.

To my husband Shane, whose facial expressions showed complete understanding of the weirdo he married after reading this, as if, "... now it all makes sense!" Your love and support mean more to me than you'll ever know.

To my children—birth and bonuses. Learn from my story. Pass it on to my grandchildren and great-grandchildren. Mamma loves!

And finally, but most importantly, because I saved the best for last, and not to sound like I've just won an Oscar – my Lord and Savior, Jesus Christ, who's been with me even before I whispered His name in the dark.

Author's Note

Flooded instantly with memories, I knew I had to write this memoir. All my life, I had talked about my past; now was as good a time as any to finally put pen to paper. It covers my earliest memories up to the present, though not necessarily in chronological order.

Please be cautioned. My story talks about physical abuse, which might be upsetting to read, especially during my and my sisters' younger years. But stay encouraged! It did not defeat us! – There's also some light language. I like to keep things real.

I hope you'll read this book all the way through to the end. And whatever emotions you feel from reading my story, I pray you'll experience joy by the time you turn the last page! Because God is in the details! He's so much more powerful than the enemy. And where God is, there is joy, no matter what the journey.

I tried to avoid clichés and adages as much as possible. But I soon gave up when I realized that the truth is simply the truth, no matter what. So, I leave you with this:

What doesn't kill you makes you stronger!

Cheezy? Yes. But it's still true!

Everyone has a story.

This is mine …

December 25, 2023

Forty-five years ago, almost to the day, three young Filipino-American sisters landed in Mississippi to live with their dad and stepmother. That was my two little sisters and me.

I had just moved back to Mississippi a few weeks ago. After settling in, I decided it was time to reach out to my stepmom, Sandy. Why not surprise her on Christmas Day?

It had been nine silent years since I last visited her—or, as I called all my unannounced visits, "checking in on her."

For the longest time, Sandy didn't have a phone. She was an off-grid recluse, living within the grid, so to speak. She had finally accepted some of life's modern amenities and got a cell phone, but I lost her number when I upgraded my phone and lost all my contacts. Sure, I could have sent her postcards to say, "Hey Sandy, I'll be in the area! I'm coming to visit!" but that just wasn't my ADD, procrastinating style. Where was the spontaneity and adventure in that? Why change my modus operandi now?

While driving to Sandy's house, I remembered that day in 1978.

I didn't know what to expect. Would I see her hobbling around with a walker? Was I about to crash a big Christmas gathering at her house? Would she scold me for taking so long to come back? Could she have dementia and not remember me?

I stepped out of the truck and stood in the unkept yard—the same yard I used to mow back in the day, with significant protest. It was the yard where I sunbathed. It was the yard I mowed while *trying* to sunbathe, and the grass clippings stuck to the tanning oil all over me.

It was quiet. No dogs barked to greet me and alert Sandy to visitors. I carefully walked up the wood-rotted steps of the front porch and knocked. I knocked again, looking around and noting the years of weathering and disrepair that a widow couldn't keep up with.

A creeping dread started to fill me. Just as I turned around, a young man was walking past the house. Shane spoke with him and asked if he knew the woman who lived there.

"Miss—Miss Sandy? You talking about Miss Sandy?" he asked.

"Yes," I called out from the porch. "I'm her daughter."

He paused. "Oh..." Then he stepped into the yard and sat on a broken statue. "Miss Sandy passed away about two or three days ago, ma'am."

Back in Arizona, when I knew we'd be moving to Mississippi, I pondered what life would be like living close to Sandy. Would our relationship grow? Would we establish the bond I had hoped to have when I was twelve? Would I bring her to my house to spend weekends with me? Would I be at her side, holding her hand as she took her last breaths, so she wouldn't die alone? That became my prayer, my request: "Father, please don't let her die alone. Let me be with her."

But just as He had said yes to me many times, today He clearly said no. I don't understand why. All I can feel right now is that I was too late. I missed her by a few days. I missed spending time with the woman my dad loved the day he died—the last link I had to him on this earth. I missed the chance to honor my dad's memory one last time by being there for his wife in her final moments. I MISSED IT!

This will haunt me.

I stood motionless for a long moment, my eyes squinting as surveyed the once-southern-landscaped front yard before I carefu took a seat on those deteriorating steps to brace myself for t barrage of memories I knew was coming.

And they hit me like an EF5 tornado.

CHAPTER 1
Mom

Once upon a lifetime ago, three little girls had a mother. She was a tiny Filipino woman with an explosive, abusive temper who married a gentle man of Scottish descent. Yes, he was in the military. Yes, she divorced him after coming to the States.

My mom loved us the best she knew how. She fed us, clothed us, sheltered us, and 'disciplined' us; all the things parents are minimally expected to do. She loved us. But she did not *like* us.

No…she did not like *me.*

As far back as I can remember, I was aware of things that most children my age were not. I was very emotionally mature. I knew what morality was before it was taught to me. But I was also dumber than a box of rocks. Not only was I not the sharpest pencil in the cup, but my lead was broken, and my eraser was chewed off. When I wasn't wise beyond my years, you could shine a flashlight through one ear and see out the other. There was no in-between with me. And this was a source of great contention for my mom. I am sure that I was the bane of her motherhood, of her very existence. I was either the voice of reason and conscience that got in the way of her nightlife and promiscuities, or I was naïve enough to get into a van with puppies and candy.

I knew that mom's infidelity while dad was out at sea was wrong.

I knew that her leaving my sisters and me home alone while she danced all night long when I was only 7 years old was wrong.

When I begged for a babysitter and couldn't find one, I knew my sisters and I sleeping in the back of the VW in the dance club parking lot, with mom saying, "Be quiet. Go to sleep. If people know you are here, they will take you away from me," was wrong.

I also knew the way she beat us was so very wrong.

When we didn't have a babysitter, I remember my sisters and I sleeping in Mom's bed while she was out dancing. The house was dark. We were scared. Listening to Mom's clock radio was the only thing that lulled us to sleep. Songs like Wildfire (Michael Murphy), The Most Beautiful Girl (Charlie Rich), and Brandy (Looking Glass) emotionally transport me back – I can still smell her room, her Avon perfume, and her hairspray.

I remember crying inconsolably when she announced to my sisters and me that she and Daddy were getting divorced. Ellen and Lulu didn't know what that meant. I don't even know how *I* knew what that meant. But Mom yelled at me to stop crying. The earth quaked under my feet that no one else felt.

Mom wished I could have gone with my dad. If I could have stowed away aboard the USS Coral Sea, I would have. That it was so easy for her to part me out while keeping my sisters was my first hint that my mother didn't like me.

THE GIRLFRIEND

We met Daddy's girlfriend during one of our weekend visits. She was nice, though she was a little greedy with her cookies. She ate cookies in front of us and didn't offer to share. When Ellen asked for a cookie, she snapped, "No!" and kept eating them. Ellen was only 8 years old. *Who does that to a child?*

When we went back home to Mom, she asked us about Dad's girlfriend.

"Oh, she's so nice and tall!" I raved. "She's got long, thick, wavy hair. She's very pretty, and she's a waitre—"

SLAP!

My face slammed to the floor. Mom slapped me so hard that my ears were ringing. W*hy??*

"SHUT UP!" Mom yelled at me. Then she mocked, "She's so pretty, she's so this, she's so that! I DON'T WANT TO HEAR YOU TALK ABOUT HER ANYMORE!"
Then why did you ask? Jealous?? Maybe you shouldn't have divorced Dad.

That was the first time I remember truly getting angry at my mom and holding it against her, down deep inside. And I knew that was wrong, too.

A few months later, Dad's girlfriend drew some pictures and mailed them to us. We complimented her art when we were at Dad's house, so she thought we'd like them. And we would have. Except Mom mailed them back to her.

SAVED

Despite Mom's nightlife, she was a semi-churchgoer and took us with her. She was a Believer in Jesus Christ, though her lifestyle said otherwise. She'd have seasons where we'd never miss a Sunday, then we'd disappear for several months.

We attended this very tiny Bible Fellowship church. When the weather was delightful, maybe 25 people would attend Sunday morning service. Mom even sang for the church! I learned about salvation at Bible Fellowship.

When I was 9, I ran up to Mom after Sunday school, so excited. "Mommy! I wanna get saved! I want to accept Jesus into my heart and get baptized!"

Mom quickly settled me down with her bulging-eyeballs glare and answered, "Not yet, Karlin. You don't understand many things. Learn more."

"I do understand, Mom!" I assured her with excitement. "I know about Adam and Eve, Noah's Ark, and Jesus dying on the cross for my sins, and then resurrected – that means coming back to life – 3 days later, so that I can belong to God and be with Him forever and ever in Heaven! I do understand!"

"Not yet. Not yet." Mom said impatiently. Then she motioned with her lips to sit in a pew "over there". It's a Filipino thing. They point with their lips.

That evening, while lying in bed, I thought, *why do I need Mom's permission to be saved? …I don't! I believe!! What more do I need to understand?*

So, I sat up in bed, in the dark, and clasped my hands together. "Jesus?..."

GO AWAY

There was a season between the 5th and 6th grades when, whenever Mom got angry with me, she wanted to send me away.

Once, she sent me to stay at a relative's house, whom I barely knew, for a week. Twice! I still can't remember their names! I remember being so homesick that I kept calling my mom, begging to come home. I didn't care how angry it would make her. I just wanted to be home, in my own bed, with my sisters and my mom, who didn't want me.

VALENTINE

Anytime I wanted to go to a friend's house, my mom's rule was that I had to arrange my transportation before going anywhere; she wanted to share the responsibility with the other parent. So, on a Saturday in February, I arranged for Mrs. Lang to drive me home if my mom would drive me there, and both moms agreed.

While at my friend Sharon's house, we made Valentine's gifts for our moms, then walked to the store and bought them small heart-shaped boxes of chocolates. On the box for my mom, I wrote, *"To the best mom in the whole world! Will you be my Valentine? – Love, Karlin."*

When it was time for me to go home, Mrs. Lang asked if my mom could pick me up because her shoulder was injured and driving was painful. *What? Why didn't you mention this earlier?!? My mom will be pissed!*

Well, thanks to my mom, my manners were impeccable; I couldn't tell Mrs. Lang no, so I made that phone call. And I was right.

On the drive home, I kept telling my mom how sorry I was that Mrs. Lang didn't fulfill her part of the arrangement and that I had no idea she had a shoulder injury. I knew Mom was mad, but she seemed to be taking it in stride. *Wow. Mom's being really understanding about all this.*

We walked down the hallway, me in front of her. I was on my way to my bedroom, and Mom to hers.

Suddenly, my chest arched in front of me, my arms flew behind me, I lost my breath, and I fell forward onto my bedroom floor.

My mom kicked me in the back so hard that it knocked the wind out of me. As I was struggling to catch my breath and sit up, she grabbed my hair and dragged me around my bedroom. She flung me to the floor. She kicked me. She slapped me repeatedly. All the while she was yelling:

I TOLD YOU TO ARRANGE TRANSPORTATION! – HOW COME SHE'S HOLDING HER BABY IF HER SHOULDER IS

HURT? – YOU CAN'T GO TO HER HOUSE ANYMORE! – HOW MANY TIMES DO I HAVE TO TELL YOU? – WHY DON'T YOU FIND SOMEWHERE ELSE TO LIVE?"

And in between slaps and hits, I answered her:

"I did, Mom," I cried. "I did ... I don't know, I don't know ..."
I nodded my head in agreement.
"I'm sorry, Mom! I'm sorry!" I cried, and I preemptively shielded my face from her hand.
"She didn't say anything about her shoulder all day." I whimpered.
And I didn't even know how to respond to her last question.

"WHAT'S IN YOUR HAND?" she yelled.

During the entire time, I clung to my mom's chocolates. I slowly raised the heart-shaped box toward her, shielding my face with my other hand.

"What's this?" she asked gruffly.

"It's your—Valentine's—Day present," I said between gasping breaths.

Mom grabbed it out of my hand and read the message on the back. Then she looked at me with red eyes and ran out of my room.

I carefully pulled my knees to my chest, hugged myself into a tight ball, and sobbed softly.
...I hate you.

I'm sorry, Lord. I know I shouldn't have said that.

My mom took out all her rage on me. I knew who she was really mad at.

But I was the one most available.

PHILIPPINES

A few weeks later, Mom mentioned sending me to the Philippines for the summer. She said she'd buy me all the clothes I wanted and that I could improve my language skills there. She described all the fun things I could do with my cousins. It sounded really fun, adventurous, and even a little grown-up. *Okay! I'll go!*

But to leave the USA, I had to get my dad's permission first, and Mom said he'd already told her no. So, Mom dictated a letter for me to write to him. After all the pleasantries, Mom had me end the letter with this:

> "… if you don't let me go to the Philippines, Dad, hatred in my heart will build up towards you."

"Mom, no!" I protested, "I'm not going to hate Dad. I don't wanna write that part."

"JUST WRITE IT!" she demanded with bulging eyes and clenched jaw. *You are so mean. You just made me lie to my dad! I'm glad he found another wife.*

About a month later, Dad called, and I answered.

"Hi, Daddy!" I exclaimed. "Are you still on the ship?"

"Yes, I am." He didn't sound like his usual self, though. "Listen, Peanut. If you want to go to the Philippines this summer, you can go." *Oh, that stupid letter!*

I looked around to see if Mom was standing over my shoulder, even though I knew she was still at work, and lowered my voice. "Daddy … I don't wanna go."

"You don't? But I thought—"

"That was Mom's idea. She made me write that letter."

"Are you sure, Peanut?"

"Yes, Daddy, I'm sure. I'm not going to hate you."

"Well, ok then. I was just afraid that your mom wouldn't bring you back, that's all."

"I know. Me too."

We said our I-love-yous and hung up.

I decided I wouldn't bring up Dad's phone call unless Mom mentioned the Philippines again. Somehow, someway, I was going to have to find the courage to stand up to her respectfully, no matter the consequences.

BLOSSOM

In June of 1978, what every adolescent girl anticipates happening finally happened to me.

I saw it on my chonies, on the toilet paper, and in the toilet bowl. I gasped. The initial, very brief moment of excitement was drowned out by a tsunami of dread, sadness, and even shame. Why shame, though? I was 12 years old and very innocent.

Mom had spoken of her teen years in the Philippines, and how my grandma was always suspicious that she would be promiscuous. The older I got, the more I sensed Mom was afraid of the same things Grandma feared. That's understandable. Except Mom either didn't know how to use it constructively to teach me, or she was just plain mean and horrible at it.

I frantically looked around the bathroom as if I could find the answer on the walls, on the towels, on the shower curtain. Then it came to me, and I called out, "ELLEN?!?" My voice amplified in the bathroom.

Ellen is my little sister, 12 months and 2 weeks younger than me. She was my spirit's non-twin twin. We look nothing alike. But many had asked if we were, and we always looked at each other with disgust, wondering which of us people thought we looked like. Me? Her?? Eww!

Ellen and I had this silent connection. Every time we got in trouble with Mom, whether we were being beaten or yelled at, Ellen and I always, always, turned to look at each other with tearful eyes. It's as if we were checking on each other. As if to say, "I know, sister." As if to convey, "I'm with you." And I'm sure we also saw in each other's eyes, "Yep, we're dead." It was our sisterly connection of support. Kind of like a lifeline to each other. But only when we were in trouble. Because any other time, I clearly liked Ellen more than she liked me.

Ellen flung open the bathroom door.

With furled eyebrows and her usual unamused expression, she flatly said, "What?"

I looked at my chonies. Ellen looked. Then we looked at each other, and I knew she knew.

"Uh oh…" she whispered. Then she called for Mom.

Mom stepped into the bathroom doorway, and Ellen pointed. "Karlin started."

Mom took a deep breath, then told Ellen to leave.

Now it was just Mom and me. She stood in the doorway in silence, staring at me. She took a few more deep breaths and then disappeared into her bedroom. I just sat there on the toilet, looking at my chonies, trying to give my inner self that blossoming-into-womanhood pep talk.

"Here! —" Mom said, as she threw a box of mini pads at me. She stared at me for a few seconds more before she disappeared into her bedroom again.

As I leaned over to pick up the box, Ellen reappeared and closed the bathroom door behind her.

"Tear that paper thing off," she whispered. "And … stick it there … I think that's how it goes."

ON THE SPOT

At the end of summer, right before 7th grade, we were all playing outside in the front yard, in the street, wherever we pleased, until the street lights came on.

Ellen, our next-door neighbor Jolie, and I were playing catch with a softball. Our other friends, Janie and Dawn, were sitting in the driveway playing jacks.

Mom opened the front door and leaned against the doorway, eating an apple, watching us.

"Hi Mom!" I called out.

"Hi, Mrs. Davis!" Jolie, Janie, and Dawn greeted almost in unison.

"Karlin, have you found a place to live yet?" Mom said nonchalantly.

I deflated. *Please, Mom, not in front of my friends.*

I caught the softball with my glove. "No— I haven't talked to anyone about it yet," I said with timidity and embarrassment. I held on to the ball, and we were all standing there quietly. Even our friends looked nervous.

Ellen and I glanced at each other, and then she looked down at the ground with a scowl that our mom couldn't see. Ellen was embarrassed, too.

"Why not?" she snapped.

"I dunno, Mom. I just—"

"Did you ask Janie?" Mom asked.

Janie startled, and her eyes got big as she patted her chest. "Me??"

"Why don't you let Karlin live with you?" Mom asked Janie before she took another bite of her apple.

"I um—I dunno. I guess I can ask my mom." Poor Janie. What an awkward spot to be put in.

I shrugged my shoulders and looked down at the ground, too. Embarrassed. Humiliated. Defeated. *Why do you do this, Mom? … I HATE YOU!!!*

I looked up at Mom. She smirked at me, shook her head, and went back into the house.

"Throw the ball, Karlin!" Ellen yelled, and everyone went back to play as if nothing had happened.

My mom did not like me.

REGRET

One Saturday afternoon, Ellen was in Mom's room, lying down with her and cuddling. Sometimes Mom was really affectionate with Ellen and Lulu.

Every time I tried to be like that with Mom, though, she would get annoyed with me, as if I were crowding her.

And truth be known, maybe I was too clingy for her. Perhaps I was the one always glomming onto her before she could be affectionate with me on her own terms.

It never hurt me to see her loving my sisters like that. But it did sting when she pushed me away.

Mom told Ellen that she regretted divorcing Daddy.

GRANDMA!

One night at dinner, Mom was shouting at Ellen and me.

As usual, we upset her over something small, like doing poorly at our piano lessons. Ellen and I exchanged our usual eye contact.

"STOP LOOKING AT EACH OTHER!!!" Mom exploded.

Ellen and I started crying.

Mom said horrible things in her anger, which made Grandma come into the kitchen to see what was wrong. Then Grandma started crying, begging her daughter to stop yelling and being mean to her granddaughters, asking, "Why are you doing dees? Why are you so mad?? Please, Anak, stop!"

Lulu then started crying, and Mom yelled at her. "How come you're crying?!?"

Lulu shrugged and cried with food in her mouth, "I dunno."

"STOP CRYING!" Mom snapped. "SHUT UP! … ALL OF YOU SHUT UP!"

Mom turned to Grandma, "WHY?!? What are you talking about?!? What do you mean by 'why'?!? … I'M LIKE THIS BECAUSE OF *YOU*!!!"

Mom argued with her own mother in Tagalog, their voices fading into the background as Ellen and I looked at each other in shock: So, this is all Grandma's fault?!?

Like in the old Godzilla movies, when the monsters fought each other, the tiny people in the foreground ran for cover. And that's exactly what we did. We scurried back to our bedrooms, out of sight.

*** *** ***

I covered my face and took a deep breath, shaking my head at these memories. Why are they taking me so far back? What does Mom have to do with Sandy?

I don't know who said it, or maybe I'm just making it up, but I heard it said that sometimes we have to go back to the beginning to understand the present. And maybe the future.

CHAPTER 2
Remembering

One time, Mom was beating Ellen and me, and we somehow ended up in our closet as we were trying to dodge her slaps.

Mom picked up a boot and kept hitting us with it while we screamed and cried, trying to shield ourselves with our hands.

Mom hit Ellen in the face with the boot. The zipper caught her bottom lip at the corner of her mouth, slicing right through it. Blood was everywhere as Ellen's lip hung. – Mom stopped. Then she yelled at me, blaming me for making her so mad that she hurt my sister.

Ellen needed stitches, but Mom tended to it herself with gauze and bandaids. Ellen was just 5 years old.

SCAR

When Ellen and Lulu were in the bathtub, Ellen poured all the bubble bath oil into the water.

Mom went into a rage and repeatedly held Ellen's head underwater.

As Ellen struggled with her arms and legs flailing, Lulu, only 2 years old, was scared and tried to get away from the commotion.

Mom let go of Ellen, grabbed Lulu, and banged her head against the bathtub rim, splitting her eyebrow open.

Most children have a scar from running into a coffee table. But not Lulu's. – You'd think after doing something like that to her toddler, Mom would have realized she had a dangerous anger problem.

BUNKBED

I only remember Ellen and me running down the hallway towards our bedroom as Mom was chasing us, whipping us with a couple of Daddy's fishing poles.

We clambered up to the top bunk and cowered against the wall in the corner, huddled together.

We screamed and cried as Mom, only 4'11", was jumping, trying to hit us with the fishing poles, but couldn't reach us.

When she finally gave up and left our room, Ellen and I started giggling quietly to each other.

HEAD BANG

Mom was … extra.

As we got older, she would bang our heads together like we were the Three Stooges whenever we argued. And she would do it in the most creative ways.

For example, when we had ponytail braids, we had to be mindful of how close we were to each other. Because if we forgot, *BANG!* Mom would yank our braids with ninja-like reflexes that knocked our heads together so hard. – One time, it sounded like our skulls cracked, and I saw stars.

God forbid if we cried, especially if we were around other people. If we did, we died when we got home.

HAIR

Anything and everything in her path and within reach became something she could use on us. Shoes, sticks, hairbrushes, oranges, toys, etc., easily became projectiles.

And heaven help us if we made Mom angry while she was doing our hair!

I lost count of how many times that pointy end of the hairbrush stabbed our backs or the top of our heads.

Or when we'd squirm because she was making our ponytails too tight. She pulled our hair so tight that we went from looking like little Filipinas to China dolls.

One time, when Mom was brushing my hair into ponies, she said, "Karlin, you're an ugly duckling. But don't worry. One day you'll grow into your beauty."

HER IDEA

When I was in the 4th grade, walking home from school, Ellen and I stopped at the Short Stop convenience store just up the road from our apartment. The same store that Mom would send me to on my bike at 9 pm with money and a handwritten note authorizing me to buy her cigarettes — Virginia Slims menthol.

I don't know why we went inside, though; neither of us had any money. But as I was looking at the basket of Bazooka bubble gum, 2 cents each, Ellen whispered in my ear, "You should steal some."

"No!" I whispered. "Shut up!"

But then … I slipped two pieces into my coat pocket and shoved another into my Cinderella lunch pail.

"Hey, you!" the cashier said to me.

"... Me?" I started to panic.

"Come here … empty your pockets … open your lunch pail," he ordered.

I did as I was told. And when he told me to stand behind the counter while he called the police, I hysterically cried, "I swear, I don't know how they got in there, sir!"

The cop car arrived, and the officer placed me in the back seat. He saw Ellen on the sidewalk and asked if she wanted a ride home, too. She said no and ran off like a chicken! THIS WAS ALL HER IDEA!

Though I didn't see her, Ellen must have beaten us home, because when the cop knocked, Mom and her boyfriend answered the door together. They never do that. They've *never* done that. Ellen must have tipped them off.

The officer told Mom I had shoplifted and handed me off to her.

I expected a beating, but didn't get one. Instead, Mom gave me the worst death stare that made me almost prefer the beating.

I think her boyfriend may have influenced her not to punish me, as if the ride in the back of the cop car was enough to teach me a lesson (which it was!). Or, she didn't want her boyfriend to see her lose control on her firstborn.

Again, for the record, *this* was Ellen's idea.

NO NEEDS

My sisters and I can laugh about some of these memories today. But the others? Even after so many years, we couldn't minimize the abuse and trauma.

Focus on the good memories, they say. But what if the bad memories seem to critically outweigh the good ones, like a fat kid on a see-saw?

Mom worked hard to support my sisters and me. Materially, we had no needs, only plenty of wants. Mom did make Christmases special with all the presents under the tree, though. But I can honestly say, I would have traded it all and lived in a cardboard box under an overpass with her, in a heartbeat, if it meant no physical and emotional abuse and having only her affection.

***

The two things Mom did right, without question, were to introduce us to the Lord and to teach us respect and manners.

Admittedly, she instilled the fear of God in us in the worst way (partial pun intended), but we knew how to mind our P's and Q's as well as any homegrown Southerner.

Later, we only had to learn the 'ma'am and sir' part.

CHAPTER 3
Ripped

December 2, 1978, was a Saturday night. I was getting ready for my junior high school Christmas dance, and Mom was getting ready for a Christmas party with some friends in the Northern California Bay Area. Ellen and Lulu were staying home with Grandma Remy.

"I don't really feel like going out tonight," Mom said to me as I was curling my feathers.

"Why?" I asked.

"I don't know. I'm just not in the mood."

"Go, Mom. Have fun."

It was a little weird encouraging my mom to go out. I mean, it's not like she was a homebody, introverted couch potato. She was actually quite the partier, and disco was her thing. However, she'd seemed a little more toned-down and mommy'er the past few months. Her airman boyfriend was stationed in Germany, which never stopped her from going out dancing, but maybe this time it did?

Mom liked my idea and went back to her room to dress up.

It was neat that the two of us were getting ready for our events at the same time. I was in the 7th grade, and Mom was 34. We were being "girly" together, something that's never happened before, simply because I wasn't old enough. But tonight, we were talking about hair, jewelry, and clothes. Mom let me put on some blush and tinted lip gloss. And for this occasion, I wore dangly earrings and pantyhose.

Mom left a few minutes before me, and I walked to my friend's house two doors down and rode with her and her mom to the dance.

Was this a coming-of-age thing between my mom and me? If so, I liked it. I liked it so very much and couldn't wait to have more moments like these with her.

NEXT DAY

The doorbell woke me up. Everyone was still sleeping, so I put my robe on and answered the door. Who was ringing our doorbell at 7 a.m. on a Sunday? *Whoa …*

"Good morning! I'm sorry to wake you up, but does Joan E. Davis live here?" the police officer asked.

I told him yes as I rubbed my eyes.

"May I talk with her, please?"

"Sure. One moment." I closed the door and walked towards Mom's room to wake her up.

Grandma Remy was standing in the hall.

"Oy! Who's dat?" she asked in her thick Filipino accent.

"A police officer wants to talk with Mom," I said.

Grandma looked confused as I opened Mom's bedroom door and saw that she wasn't in her bed.

It wasn't uncommon for Mom to pull all-nighters when she went out dancing. Or for her to come home late, get a few hours of sleep, and go in early on the weekend to work some overtime. Even though Mom's bed looked exactly like it did yesterday, I went with the latter explanation of why she wasn't home.

"Ees your mom sleeping?" Grandma asked as I passed her in the hallway and went back to the front door.

"No, Grandma. I think she went to work."

I opened the door to the police officer and apologized that my mom wasn't home, like I thought.

"Is there something wrong, sir?" I asked.

The officer removed his cover, and his smile turned flat.

"Are there any other adults in the home?" he asked with seriousness.

"My grandmother is here. Hold on—"

I motioned to Grandma. She zipped up her robe and came to the door.

"Good morning, ma'am. My name is Officer Johnson. May I talk with you for a moment, please?" Grandma Remy stepped outside, and the officer closed the front door behind her.

I stood in the entrance way, wondering, listening, and waiting. The officer's voice was low, and he spoke slowly as Grandma grew increasingly panicked. Then she wailed.

"OOOOOOOOOY!!! She's gone? Joan ees gone??"
Mom's gone? Where did she go? Did she run off with some guy?!?

I flung open the front door, and Grandma was crying.

"What's going on?!?" my 12-year-old self demanded. "What happened?!?"

"Your mom! She's gone! Oyyyyyyy! Your mom ees gone, Karlin!" Grandma cried.

"What??? Where?!? Where did she go?!?"

Then the officer put his hand on my shoulder. "Ma'am, there was a car accident very early this morning. We believe one of the passengers is Joan Davis…"

"How do you know?" I demanded.

Grandma kept crying.

The officer showed me Mom's driver's license. "Is this your mom?"

"YES!" I started to panic. My voice didn't sound like mine. "WHERE IS SHE?"

"I'm sorry," the officer said. And now his eyes had filled with tears, "She … Your mom … passed."

I stared at him incredulously for the longest 3 seconds. "Passed? What– What does that mean?"

The officer hesitated, "…Your mom died earlier this morning in a car accident."

The Earth's rotation came to a jolting stop. The air was heavy, and it felt hard to breathe. Daylight turned dim. Voices sounded muffled. Everything was wrong.

"What? What??—" I screamed, " WHAT???— WHAT?!?— WHAAAAAAAAT?!?" I kept screaming. Because if I stopped, it would be real.

Grandma, the officer, and I ended up back in the house. Ellen met us in the entranceway and started crying hysterically.

Standing by herself in the hallway was 9-year-old little Lulu, crying. "Why is everyone crying?"

Dead. Our mom was dead. The house was filled with hysteria. And the police officer was trying to console us all. But inside me, there was nothing. Just … life-stealing shock.

My memory of that horrible day is like broken glass. Sharp. And I remember shards of it. Large shards. And there were a lot. But I have not forgotten the complete ripping apart of my world.

She was meaner than a devil. She hurt us. She scared us. But she was *my* mom. She was all I knew.

I knew she was wrong about many things, many times. I knew her mothering was far from ideal and fell short of the standard. I knew in my heart there was a better way and always hoped for it.

She was my world. I loved her. And now she was gone. No more. How do three young girls live without their mother?

Even now, forty-five years later, that memory hasn't faded.

Not even a little.

Mom's sister, Aunty Suzette, arrived from Germany, and Mom's attorney came to the house.

They were having an adults-only conversation with the other family members who had shown up, which I mindlessly walked into. I entered at exactly the moment someone mentioned foster care and separating my sisters and me. I was 12, I knew my manners, and I probably misheard the whole conversation, but that day, I didn't care. I raised my voice.

"We will not be separated!" I declared. "I don't know what to do, but no one is going to tear us apart!"

I'm not sure where this boldness came from, but it appeared, and probably looked like a hissing kitten.

The grown-ups were quiet. Someone notified the Red Cross, which informed the US Navy, which advised my dad.

Daddy was on his way.

***

Mom's death was accidental, but at 34, she already had her affairs in order. I still don't know if that was impressive or creepy. She was very organized. She had a will, and I knew who Mom wanted us to go to if this happened. But we had to find the will.

CHAPTER 4
The Funeral

Even with a house full of relatives, it was quiet. It was as if everyone were deliberately talking as little as possible, almost in whispers, deep in thought.

I remember lying in my bed, looking up at the ceiling, when my friend Janie came over. Her freckled face with strawberry blonde hair, popped into my view as she looked down at me and whispered, "Oh my gosh, Karlin. As I was walking down the hallway, I saw Lulu in your mom's bedroom, sitting at her big makeup mirror. She was playing your mom's ukulele and singing to her picture." – Lulu didn't know how to play the ukulele.

Dad and Sandy arrived. And what an entrance that was.

Dad was dad. But Sandy? Wedged heels, shiny pantyhose, super short wool skirt, long-sleeved white ribbed turtleneck sweater, no bra, giant sunglasses, and thick, wavy, chestnut-with-highlights long hair like the mane of a wild mustang.

All the Filipinos briefly stared. Aunty Suzette curled her lip. But Mom's cousin, Uncle Winston, broke the silence and greeted my dad with a handshake and familiar cordiality, "Brother Jim!"

Sandy held on to Daddy's other hand tightly.

"You did what?!?" Aunty Suzzette said, trying to whisper.

I overheard – Ok, I eavesdropped – on her and Grandma's conversation about sleeping arrangements.

"Anak, dat's Jim," Grandma reasoned. "Op course I'm going to let him sleep in Joan's room."

Auntie Suzzette was trying to contain herself. "But her?... HER? … Mommy, no!"

"It's too late—he ees already in dair," Grandma stood firm.

Auntie Suzette needed a break from all the legal conversations and went for a walk. When she returned to the house, Sandy was roller-skating up and down the sidewalk in front of it. Auntie Suzette thought that was such odd behavior for an adult woman, especially given the somber occasion.

GRAVE SITE

We rode in the limo to the funeral home with Dad and Sandy.

Your eyes play tricks on you when looking at a dead person. I got to the front row of the pews and stopped. I looked at Mom for a long time from where I stood.

"She looks like she's sleeping," I said aloud.

"Yes, she is sleeping for now," Auntie Suzzette said as she walked up behind me and stroked my hair before going to her pew.

Lulu walked up beside me, and together we walked the rest of the way to her casket.

Mom was dressed in a yellow traditional Filipino dress with flared butterfly sleeves. I thought it was lovely, but Lulu thought it was ugly. Her makeup was definitely horrid. Someone painted her eyelids with a chalky pastel blue eyeshadow, blushed her cheeks with bright pink, and probably used the same for her lips. Were they going for a Barbie look? I guess no one thought to ask her eldest daughter about her makeup.

Dad and Sandy were in the front row with the rest of us. Everyone was quiet, respectful, and whispering, as Sandy stood tall, somewhat smirking, keeping her gaze forward through her sunglasses.

Nearby, Auntie Suzette was scowling as she comforted Grandma. Sure, she was Brother Jim's wife, and everybody got along well with Daddy, but Sandy was not part of us. Not according to Auntie Suzette.

Ellen sat next to Daddy. She was pretty stoic for an 11-year-old.

As she observed Mom, only able to see the side of her face and jet-black hair above the rim of the casket, Ellen had thoughts. She, too, did not like Mom's makeup. And she was relieved that she did not have to experience her first period with her. Then she looked up at

Daddy and saw tears streaming down his face. Ellen took his hand. She didn't cry at Mom's funeral.

At the cemetery, everyone ceremoniously dropped flowers onto Mom's casket. Lulu was handed a gladiolus stalk. She looked at it for a moment, then gently removed each flower one by one and let them drop.

Apparently, Lulu was moving too slowly for Ellen's liking, so Ellen rolled her eyes and scolded impatiently, "Just throw the whole thing in there!"

"No!" Lulu refused.

Ellen tried to snatch the stalk from her, but Lulu held on to it for dear life.

There my little sisters were, standing at Mom's gravesite, engaged in a back-and-forth tug of war over a stalk of gladiolas while they whisper-argued. Lulu wouldn't let go. But eventually, Ellen won and threw the now-broken stalk onto the casket.

After the funeral, we all went back to the house, where all the Filipinos did what they do best on any occasion. EAT! Every flat surface in the house was used as a table to hold plates and dishes, and aluminum foil containers filled with mouthwatering, glorious Filipino food. Everyone ate and fellowshipped. The mood even seemed uplifted.

Then there was this plate of food set in front of an empty chair at the dining table. I asked Grandma whose plate that was.

"Dat ees por your mom," she said reverently, as she ushered me into another room with all the guests.

Ellen was talking with Dad and Sandy.
"... You were crying, Daddy," she blurted.

"No, I wasn't, Monster," he denied. "I had something in my eye."

Sandy heard Ellen, and she whipped her head around and gave Daddy a disapproving glare.

It was rumored that Dad and Sandy found Mom's will and tore it up. Whatever was in it, no one will ever know aside from hearsay.

Christmas 1978. We hugged our grandma Remy goodbye. We were ripped out of our Filipino culture in California – everything that was Mom to us – and Daddy took his three daughters back to Mississippi.

*** *** ***

"Karlin? … Karlin??"
I blinked. Shane was calling my name.

"I'm so sorry, Sweetheart," he said, standing in front of me, holding out his hand. I took his hand and stood up.

"Are you OK?" he asked me.

I thought for a moment. "Yeah, I'm OK," I said, unsure of my own answer. "I just don't know what to feel right now."

Shane escorted me to the car, and we drove home. For 90 miles, my memories played like a movie in my head.

CHAPTER 5
Daddy

Daddy was a simple man. He was a soft-spoken man. He was a very kind and gentle man. I don't know if he wanted any sons, but he ended up with three daughters.

He taught his girls how to hunt and dress wild game, fish, clean it, and sleep under the stars. He involved us in his auto mechanics, his woodworking, and even put us on a tin roof to paint it.

He named us Karlin, Ellen, and Lulu (short for LuVerna). But he called us Peanut, Monster, and Wow as if those were the names on our birth certificates. Sibling rivalry for us was about who got to go deer hunting with Daddy.

I don't know where my nickname, Peanut, came from. I told stories like, "When I was born, I looked like a peanut" and "When I was little, I loved peanuts" because I wanted to have a story – any story, like everyone else – about the origin of my nickname. So, yeah, I don't know where it came from.

But Monster? That's because Ellen was the brother that Lulu and I never had. Her story goes like this: Daddy was watching Ellen play when she was little, and he muttered to my Uncle Sammy (Mom's brother), "… I think Ellen was born with the wrong parts."

And Wow? That came from baby Lulu being dressed up so cute with bows and ruffles, and being instructed by Mom to go show Daddy, to which Lulu toddled out to him, turned a circle, and waited for Daddy to say "Wow!"

SPANKED

I was 4 years old when I witnessed Daddy use brute force for the first and only time.

I woke up to our housegirl, Nina, standing over me, fretting over the commotion that was going on in the living room, right outside my door.

I sat up in bed, heard the noise, then walked to the doorway.

"Oy, Karlin! No, no, no. Stay here with me," she whispered as she tried to reach for me.

Mom was in a crying fit, breaking empty liquor bottles that were once used as decorations, while wrestling with Daddy. I couldn't understand what Mom was yelling about, but while Daddy was trying to get his grip on her, I understood what he said:

"Joan! … if you're going to act like a child … you're going to … get spanked like one!"

Needless to say, Mom strongly disagreed.

I stood in the doorway, rubbing my eyes, watching them. They didn't even notice me. But sure enough, Daddy finally got Mom over his knees and commenced to spanking her.

Nina was lying in my bed, so I crawled in with her and we cuddled until I fell asleep.

MARRY ME

They say a girl's first love is her Daddy.

In the Philippines, I remember waking up before sunrise to the aroma of bacon, eggs, and coffee. That was Daddy's breakfast before going to work. He'd sit at the dining table, dressed in his Navy dungarees, reading the newspaper while having his coffee.

I remember sitting on his lap before he left one morning, hugging him and kissing him. At 5 years old, I remember studying his face. I even asked my dad to marry me.

"Daddy, when you come home from work, let's get married."

"I can't, Peanut." Daddy chuckled.

"How come?"

"Because I'm already married to your mom."

"Oh. Her…" I don't know what I meant by that, I just remembered saying it, and Daddy laughing as he kissed my forehead, pinched my nose goodbye, and left for work.

I guess they're right.

FIREPLACE

It was a cold autumn evening in Northern California. Daddy had just built a fire in the fireplace, and the two of us were sitting in front of it, enjoying the warmth.

10 minutes later, Mom came out of the kitchen with the trash and threw it in the fireplace.

Daddy tried to stop her, "Joan! Stop! No, no, no! You can't burn that kind of stuff in a fireplace, honey!"

Mom yelled at him, "SHUT UP! It's a fire, isn't it? I CAN BURN IT THEN!"

Then I chimed in, "Mom … it stinks now.'

"SHUT UP!!!" She yelled before going back to the kitchen.

I looked at Daddy, who was just sitting there, staring into the fire, looking defeated and helpless, and ignoring that I was staring at him.

Don't let her talk to you like that, I thought. Stand up to her! Someone has to!

I hated that my mom treated Daddy like that. And I hated that Daddy let her.

At 7 years old, I was disappointed in his weakness.

THE HITCHIKER

Dad was headed back to the Navy base. It was almost 2 a.m.

While driving over a bridge, Dad saw a man walking along the curb, as there were no sidewalks. Step on the curb, step on the road, back and forth, awkwardly up and down. This bridge was not safe for pedestrians. Dad wondered if his car had broken down, and that's why he was walking.

Picking up hitchhikers was becoming taboo back then. And though he wasn't thumbing for a ride, he was still considered a hitchhiker. But Dad pulled up anyway and asked the guy if he needed a ride, or at least to get off the bridge and go somewhere safer.

"What?" He spoke. "Why?" and he flung his hair over her shoulder. "... So you can rape me and kill me and throw my body into the ocean?" She said gruffly, "No, thank you. I'm fine," and kept walking. *A woman?!?*

"What?? I wouldn't do that! I'm just offering to get you off the bridge, lady; it's not safe," he assured while rolling slowly beside her.

"Yeah, right! That's what they all say!" She rolled her eyes, flung her hair again, and kept walking.

"Oh, c'mon. Let's just get you off this bridge," Dad encouraged. "You're going to get hit; I barely saw you myself."

The woman ignored Dad and kept walking, while he slowly followed along.

"Fine!" she said and stopped abruptly, as if she'd just lost the argument with herself.

As she was getting into my dad's truck, she mumbled, "Oh, why not? Can't be any worse than the original plan."

They ended up talking for hours, and Dad dropped her off at a friend's house.

Her name was Sandy.

Dad's brother once said, "If your dad saw a wounded animal on the side of the road, he would pull over and help it. And if he believed there was the slightest chance he could nurture it back to health, he would take it home and do so."

The original plan? Sandy was walking that bridge, looking for a spot to jump off.

CHAPTER 6
Sandy

At eighteen, Sandy left home in Big Springs, TX, and hitchhiked to San Francisco, CA.

Haight-Ashbury was the hippie mecca, and a hippie, Sandy was. Free love. Freedom. No rules. She fit right in.

She was a tall woman with thick, long, wavy brown hair, one length and parted down the middle like a curtain. Her face was scarred by teen acne, but it didn't take away from the beauty of her strong Cherokee features.

She met my dad on a bridge at 2 a.m. and 10 months later, married him.

Some time in her early twenties, Sandy needed a full hysterectomy. She asked my dad about adopting a child, but my dad said no, "I already have three girls. I don't want any more."

"But *I* don't have any, Jim," she reasoned. "Wouldn't it be nice for you and me to have our own, together?"

"My girls can be your girls, too," Daddy said, not really hearing what his wife's heart was saying.

"It's not the same, Jim." Sandy felt rejected.

She became our stepmother the day she married my dad in 1976. But when we moved to Mississippi, she went from being "Dad's wife" to something else. Something more permanent.

Despite the bad rap fairytales give them, I was willing to give my stepmom a chance. Of course, I knew Sandy could never—would never—take Mom's place. But she was in a "mom" position … and we had just lost ours … and three young, adolescent girls could use a mom person in their lives, right? … so why not embrace it?

Looking back at our lives with Mom, I mean, how bad could this new life be? We were with Daddy now, our protector. He was nothing like Mom. So, what could go wrong? This was my 12-year-old self being wise beyond my years.

At first, it was small things. Easy to dismiss. But after about two weeks of this new family stuff, I began noticing a grumpiness in Sandy.

It started when we were all wrestling around in the living room, the girls against Dad. In the middle of all the squealing and laughter, I just happened to notice some grays in Daddy's hair and mentioned it.

"Daddy, you're getting gray!" I noted playfully.

He brushed it off. "Yep, that's what happens when you get old, Peanut," and kept wrestling with us without skipping a beat.

But Sandy stopped playing and pulled me aside.

"Karlin, you don't say things like that to your dad!" she growled. "That's rude!"

I was confused and shocked.

"How was that rude?" I asked. "Up until my mom died, I didn't see Dad very often, and I'm just now noticing. I've also never even seen the top of Daddy's head before!" I explained.

"Well, what if your dad said something about your period?" She lowered her voice to a coarse whisper. *Whoa! Whoa! Whoa! What??*

"... I dunno," I replied, my eyes darted around incredulously looking for an answer. "Why would he? It's not even the same thing!"

That was so weird.

Not too long after that incident, Sandy reacted to my pajamas and made a new rule. She announced that I had to be fully dressed whenever I left my bedroom.

I looked down at my jammies. My poofy, ruffled,
"Little House on the Prairie - trying to look modern but failed" jammies.

"Um … Ok." I accepted.

For a moment, I felt immodest and ashamed. But then I quickly realized that the bloomers of my jammies were more modest than my school-issued gym shorts. *But OK. Whatever.*

RICE

My sisters and I went from eating rice three times a day to barely eating any at all. So, one afternoon, I made some rice on the stove top. I even found some spam. Just a teency taste of the old home was all we wanted. However, having only ever used a rice cooker, I burnt some of the rice at the bottom of the pot. We still ate rice and spam, though!

When Sandy came home, she was so irate to see the pot soaking in the sink.

"WHO DID THIS?!?" She came to my room with the pot of burnt rice stuck to the bottom.

"I did," I said. "I'm sorry, I burnt the bottom. I've never cooked rice like that before."

"LOOK AT ALL THIS WASTED RICE!" She harped. "IF YOU CAN'T COOK RICE, DON'T COOK AT ALL!"

"I *can* cook rice, but—"

"STAY OUT OF THE KITCHEN, KARLIN!" *Geeeeeez, OK! Is this really a big deal?*

CHURCH

In Mississippi, everyone goes to church. You're kind of a weirdo if you don't. I was invited to a youth group at a local Baptist church, so I decided to go. I made friends and joined the youth choir. When I wasn't at home, I was at church. After losing your mom just a few months ago, there really is no better place to be than church. It was also my escape. My refuge. And it was the only place I felt… normal.

So she took it away. If I wanted to go, I had to earn it. More chores. Perfectly done. If I missed something, I couldn't go. Isn't there a Disney princess with this dilemma?

The fussing was never-ending. Sandy kept calling me a spoiled brat, reminding me how unpopular I was at school, and telling me I was deceitful like my mother. And her favorite? That I was so vain. – Still a child myself, but without the fear of my mom, I argued back. It was almost as if she was trying to evoke the same hurtful feelings someone else once caused her.

So, to discipline me for dissenting, the only thing they could take away from me—since there was nothing else—was church. The one place I felt safe became conditional.

I never talked back to my mom or anyone else, for that matter. That was disrespectful. But I was becoming increasingly disrespectful toward Sandy and, unintentionally, toward Daddy.

RULES JUST FOR ME

One Saturday morning, I sleepily changed out of my jammies and went to the kitchen for breakfast. Sandy immediately halted me.

"Uh, NO! Go back to your room, Karlin, and put on a bra!"

I looked down.

"Oops. I'm sorry," I said in a yawn, and turned to go back to my room.

"You're getting too old to walk around without a bra ... YOU LOOK LIKE A WHORE!"

I paused. *What???* I turned back around.

"…*You* don't wear a bra," I pointed out.

"I DON'T HAVE TO! I'M 29 YEARS OLD! I'M MARRIED!" Sandy justified.

"…DOESN'T MEAN EVERYONE WANTS TO SEE YOUR NIPPLES!" I fired back.

Daddy sent me to my room for the rest of the morning.

I think Daddy started to realize my struggle. For my thirteenth birthday, he bought me the books, The Hobbit, and The Lord of the Rings trilogy set. I lost myself in Middle Earth as much and as often as I could.

She called me a whore in front of my dad!

MOTHER'S DAY

Mother's Day rolled around. It was our first one without Mom. Lulu's elementary class made cards for their mothers. She explained to her teacher that she had no one to give her card to because our mother was dead, but it fell on deaf ears, and she was instructed to make a card anyway.

So little Lulu brought hers home and gave it to Sandy.

Sandy looked at it, then handed it back to her.

"I'm not your mother," she said and went into her bedroom.

OH NO YOU DIDN'T!

I could not believe her cold, rotten heart. I couldn't believe my dad married *that*! I stared at Sandy intently as she walked past me, hoping she would see my glare and say something. Anything. I wanted an excuse to call her horrible things. My poor baby sister! *Hurt me all you want, but don't you dare hurt my baby sister!*

PASSIVE

I was making my dinner plate to join the family around the dinette. I can't remember what Sandy said, or what my response was. But Sandy jumped up from her chair, grabbed my arm, spun me around, grabbed my neck, and bent me backward over the kitchen sink. I thought my spine was going to snap! I don't even remember what she threatened me with, but she growled it.

Whatever I said didn't cause a reaction from Dad, so I didn't understand why Sandy reacted the way she did.

As Ellen watched, she said, "Dad?" and nudged him with her elbow, as if to ask whether he was going to do anything about it. But he kept eating his dinner.

I learned in that moment that my dad was so gentle, he was weak. I recognized his passivity from when he was married to Mom.

I was wrong for my disrespect. But from my 13-year-old eyes, I was tired of being picked on, being singled out, and being bullied. Sandy was an equal-opportunity offender, but she clearly had it out for me.

Our arguments and screaming matches were progressing in pitch and frequency by the week, so Daddy – with Sandy's input: "Something's wrong with that girl!" – arranged for the three of us to talk to a counselor on the base.

"Great," I smirked. "My parents think I'm crazy."

The counselor talked with me first.

"My mom died 9 months ago; 2 weeks later, my sisters and I left my Grandma and everything we knew, and moved to Mississippi… I thought Sandy would be a good, friendly mom… I like going to the church youth group… I like to read and draw, and go hunting and fishing with my dad… Sandy keeps calling me names, putting me down, and picking fights with me. I don't understand why—I do what I'm told... I know I'm being disrespectful when I talk back to her, but I feel like I have to defend myself... I *know* when I do wrong and deserve discipline... I do like to wear make-up 'cause I feel pretty, but Sandy won't let me, so I sneak it. I know I'm wrong for that. But why not just let me wear a little?... I don't smoke, I don't drink, I don't sneak out. We don't even watch TV because they moved it into their bedroom… All we do are chores and homework, and when I'm done, I read or draw… Oh, and Sandy told my sisters and me that, even though my dad keeps telling us she loves us very much, she doesn't. Sooooo …"

We talked for a long time.

Then it was Dad's and Sandy's turn. They weren't with the counselor very long.

As we were walking to the car, I asked, "So, what's wrong with me?"

Dad spoke lowly, "Nothing's 'wrong' with you, Peanut."

"He's a quack!" Sandy exclaimed indignantly.
Of course, you'd say that.

I guess they didn't like what the counselor said? If I could have been a fly on that wall, I'm willing to bet their conversation went something like this:

"Cut Karlin some slack. Let her finish the grieving process. Sandy, it sounds like you've got some pent-up aggression from your own past that you need to work through. How about I see you next week?"

HAIRCUT

That summer, Sandy came into my bedroom with scissors.

"Come on. You're getting a haircut!" she demanded.

I put my book down. "What? … Why? … I don't need a haircut." *How random!*

"I don't care," she said. "When I was your age, I had to get my hair cut off. Besides, it's summer, it's humid, and you won't be able to manage your hair." *Yes, I can!*

"What does your haircut have to do with my hair? Daddy likes my long hair anyway."

"Come on, let's go!" Sandy insisted.

"… No," I said low and firm.

Sandy slammed my door and stomped away. I went looking for Dad and found him outside working on his truck.

"Daddy, do I have to get a haircut?" I asked.

"No, Peanut. Why?"

"Sandy wants to cut my hair."

"She does?"

"Do you like my hair, Daddy?"

"Of course I do, Peanut."

Then I ran back inside as soon as Sandy spotted us talking.

Based on her body language, she was not happy at all. The childish me was pleased to have beaten her at her stupid game.

BAPTIZED

Despite all the punishments, I did manage to get baptized! And Dad and Sandy came to church for it!

Just moments before I was dunked, Dad and Sandy walked through the doors and took their seats near the front.

Daddy wore his Navy dress blues without the jacket and was very handsome. He made eye contact with me and winked.

Sandy wore tight, satin coral-pink pants with a matching zip-up jacket. *Oh my …*

She looked uncomfortable – either because she didn't have anything "churchy" to wear, or she was worried the paint would peel and the Bible would spontaneously combust, revealing her true nature.

CHAPTER 7
Life

This was our life now. It was so uncomfortable – hostile, defensive, angry, bitter, resentful. A constant struggle. Unlike with Mom, I couldn't just make a phone call and beg to come home. This was home now. And every day brought its own dark cloud, regardless of the forecast…

CASTOR OIL

On a beautiful Saturday morning, Sandy called us into the kitchen. She was holding a dark bottle in one hand and a tablespoon in the other. Then she poured a thick, pale-yellow liquid onto the spoon.

"What is that?" Lulu asked.

"This is" Sandy carefully poured, "… castor oil."

"What's it for?" Ellen asked.

"This will help clean your gut out," Sandy said. *My gut doesn't need cleaning out.*

I looked at my sisters. Lulu and I made eye contact. Ellen kept looking forward.

Sandy slowly brought the spoon to my mouth, "Open wide," she said.

As soon as I swallowed it, my body contorted. *Blahhhhhhh!*

Ellen swallowed her spoonful and shuddered. Lulu kept gagging her spoonful up, and Sandy laughed wickedly until she kept it down.

What Sandy failed to explain was that "help clean your gut out" actually meant we'd be enduring obnoxious stomach gurgling, double-over intestinal cramps, and explosive diarrhea—all day—in a one-bathroom trailer. Our farts were so atomic, we couldn't trust them. *What kind of voodoo was this?!?*

We stayed huddled in the hallway, waiting for the toilet and begging the current occupant to hurry up. With clenched butt cheeks, we writhed in pain and scratched and clawed at the bathroom door while Sandy laughed maniacally from her bedroom. Our sphincters were on fire!

When it was my turn on the commode, while expelling liquid fire from my southern region, I had an idea. I remembered hearing someone say that cheese and too much bread could cause constipation. I didn't want a blockage; we just needed a serious speedbump. I knew we had cheese slices, bread, and butter.

<gasp> GRILLED CHEESE SANDWICHES!

What could it hurt? When I finished with my current bout, I let a sister in and ran to the kitchen. Time was of the essence.

As Sandy heard my clatter in the kitchen, she came to inspect.

"What are you doing?" She inquired.

"I'm making grilled cheese sandwiches for us."

"Why?"

"Because we can't all three use the toilet at the same time," I said with maybe a hint of annoyance.

She smirked and returned to her bedroom. She was enjoying this too much.

When I used up all the butter, we just ate the cheese and bread.

I don't know if I misunderstood what I heard about cheese and bread, or if it was just bad information, but … all it did was fuel our acid poops. My sisters and I stayed camped out in the hallway, never venturing too far from the toilet. I caught several cramps in my gluteals from hyperclenching.

When Daddy came home and saw us covered in blankets and lying on pillows around the bathroom door, he asked what was going on. "I gave them castor oil today," Sandy answered.

Daddy chuckled, "That'll do it."

The next day, after our intestinal turmoil ended, Ellen said that Sandy had noticed how long it was taking her to go #2.

"So YOU'RE the one that's constipated?!?" I asked with irritation.

"—I guess," Ellen replied and shrugged.

"Then why didn't she just give it to YOU?!?"

"Yeah?!?" Lulu chimed in on my side.

GLASSES

It could have been hereditary, or it could have been all those late-night readings of J.R.R. Tolkien books by flashlight under the blankets, but I was having trouble focusing my vision. So Daddy took Ellen and me to get our eyes checked on base.

Ellen stepped in front of me, "I'll go first!" She announced.

When it was my turn, I looked into the eye chart device thingy. All I saw was a strip of blur.

"Can you read the letters for me, please?" asked the optometrist.

"I—I can't see any letters," I said.

"What?!?" Ellen exclaimed. "You're lying!"

"I'm serious. I just see a blurry line of something." I said.

After more testing, we learned that I needed glasses.

As I sat in the dimly lit exam room, the doctor explained how important it was for me to wear my eyeglasses every day. *Ok.* If I didn't, over time, my vision would get worse, and I could go blind. *What? My eyes are that bad??* And, that I'm going to have to not care about how I look because my vision is more important. *Hmmm. That sounded oddly familiar.*

As I picked out eyeglasses that I knew I'd wear every day, Sandy kept saying no to all of them. I sighed with frustration. Then Sandy picked up a frame.

"How about this one?" and she held it up to my face.

"Those are ugly," I said. "And it has Battlestar Galactica on it."

"So?" She held it up to my face again.

Ellen took a step back from everyone and pointed at me, silently jeering. She laughed at the Battlestar Galactica brand, too.

"I'm not into Battlestar Galactica, Sandy. I never have been. And I'm 13. PLEASE!" I reasoned.

"Nope. You're getting these."

I looked at my dad. "Daddy?" I pleaded.

"Peanut, you look fine in them. You're beautiful no matter what."

Sandy smirked.

I KNEW IT! She wants me to go blind! She just made sure I wouldn't wear these ugly glasses in public. She set me up!!

Ellen jeered some more.

MY HERO

I didn't do purses in junior high, and back then, we didn't do bookbags. So, I'd stuff maxi pads in my tube socks and stash them in my locker when I got to school. Of course, Murphy's Law, I had an accident at school and hadn't replenished my supplies. I had no other feasible options, so I wrapped my jacket around my waist and went to the school office to call my dad at work.

"Daddy?" I cringed. "I need to get a hold of Sandy. It's really important. Can you drive home and tell her to answer the phone?"

I knew this request was absolutely absurd, but I didn't know what else to do. Sandy worked the night shift at the hospital and turned off the ringer during the day so she could sleep.

"Peanut, what's the matter?" Daddy asked so gently.

"Daddy, I just need Sandy, please. Please? Can you get a hold of her? Please?" I was getting desperate.

"Peanut?" Daddy emphasized with gentleness. "Tell me what you need."

"No. I can't. I just need Sandy. Please, Daddy?"

"It's ok, Peanut. You can tell me. I'm your father."

"Pleeeeeeeeeeeeease, Daddy!"

"Peanut? … Peanut??"

I took a deep breath and let out a long sigh.

"Fine…" I buckled.

Then I covered the phone's mouthpiece and mumbled, "I need some maxi pads." I covered my face and shook my head. I wanted to be invisible.

"And where are they?" Daddy was as calm and gentle as a quiet mountain stream. With birds chirping. And butterflies fluttering around. And a deer drinking water.

"In my bedroom, in a box in a basket covered by a blanket, next to my desk," I muttered.

"Ok. I'll see you in a little bit."

"Wait! Daddy? … Just—Just don't make it look obvious, ok? Like, just—"

"I know what to do, Peanut. Don't worry."

"… and sweatpants!" I added.

It was a rainy day, so PE was in the gym. I was sitting on the bleachers with my classmates when I saw my dad come in through the double doors. I ran to him. He handed me a brown paper bag that looked like lunch, and a pair of rolled-up sweats. When I peeked inside, I was so relieved.

"Thanks, Dad!" I said and turned to run to the locker room.

Daddy caught my arm. "I love you, Peanut," he whispered. Then he kissed the top of my head and left.

When I rejoined my classmates on the bleachers, they asked, "Who was that?"

"That's my Daddy," I said proudly.

He was a flawed man. But he had just become my hero.

I got a little sassy with my 8th-grade teacher, so she wrote a letter to my parents and sent it home with me to give to them. I read it on the bus ride home from school.

Weirdly, Dad and Sandy were sitting in the living room, as if waiting for us to come home from school, which they've never done. So I handed them the letter, and they read it.

Sandy said, "The letter's been opened."

I said, "I know. I read it."

Dad said, "It wasn't addressed to you, Peanut."

"I know. But it was about me."

"But it wasn't addressed to you," Sandy said.

"But it was about ME."

"But it's not addressed to you, Karlin," Sandy said sharply.

"But it was ABOUT ME."

"It's against the law to open mail that isn't addressed to you!" She growled.

"Huh? … It is??"

"YES! IT IS!" Sandy yelled.

"Ok. Sorry."

I admit, I was a little flippant. But my 13-year-old self simply couldn't understand what the big deal was. I still gave them the letter after all. I could have thrown it out the bus window. Which I'm sure my teacher took into consideration, which explains why my parents were waiting for me.

I was being rebellious. I kept wearing makeup at school when Sandy clearly said I wasn't allowed to. I was sassing back when Sandy singled me out and picked on me; I stood my ground. So, to quell my uprising and break my will, Daddy needed to discipline me.

About an hour later, Daddy called me out to the backyard. Sandy was holding a walking stick that looked freshly whittled from a tree branch.

Daddy said, "Come here, Peanut," and he opened his arms. I went in for the hug, and he held me tight. I thought we were going for a walk to talk about my attitude and disrespect.

"You need to be disciplined", Daddy said in my ear.

"What?"

WHACK!
I yelled out in pain, in shock. Daddy locked his arms around me.

WHACK! WHACK! WHACK! Sandy struck the back of my thighs with her stick.

I screamed and tried to break free from my dad's hold.
WHACK! WHACK!

"Daddy?!?" I cried, "NOOOOOOO!!!"

WHACK! WHACK! WHACK! Sandy changed hands.

"OH MY GOD, OH MY GOD, STOP!!! ...PLEASE, PLEASE STOP! ...OK, OK, OK!!!" I wailed and begged.

I felt all of Sandy's resentment, all her bitterness, all her hate for me with every whip. I felt her satisfaction in hurting me with every strike.

WHACK! WHACK! WHACK! Sandy changed hands again.

"OK! OK! I'M SORRY!!!" I screamed. "I'M SORRYYYYYYYY!!!"

Cars drove by. But no one stopped.

I wrestled to break free but couldn't.

WHACK! WHACK! WHACK! Sandy changed hands yet again. WHACK! WHACK! WHACK!

I wailed one last time before my knees buckled, and Daddy was holding all my weight. My arms went limp, and my head rolled back.

"Ok … I'm sorry … I'm sorry, Daddy," I sobbed.

Sandy raised her stick again, but my dad said, "That's enough."

Sandy disappeared, but Daddy held me. My long black hair was disheveled and matted to my tear-soaked face, smeared with snot as I sobbed so hard trying to catch my breath.

In the bathroom, I carefully peeled off my corduroy bellbottoms and stepped into some gym shorts. I could only sit on the edge of the toilet seat. Bleeding welts covered the back of my thighs. I dropped my head and quietly sobbed some more.

Daddy came in and saw my legs. I looked up at him through swollen eyes.

"I did not like doing that, Peanut," he said in his soft-spoken tone, as he brushed my hair out of my face and behind my left ear.

"I know, Daddy," I whispered hoarsely. "But it should have been you. At least you love me."

Sandy came into the bathroom, demanding to know what was going on. I didn't realize how much I'd let my guard down around Daddy until I put it back up when she walked in. Daddy asked if Sandy could tend to my legs, and she huffed, "With what, Jim?"

Sandy rummaged through the medicine cabinet like a brat having a hissy fit. I just could not understand how she could hate me so much.

She instructed me to stand on the toilet seat and began applying a white cream to the back of my legs. "All I've got is face cream."

To say I was heartbroken that my hero allowed this is a gross understatement. I felt so abandoned, so betrayed. What's worse? This, or Mom's rage? *I feel so alone, Lord. I feel so alone.*

That was on a Friday. By Monday, my welts were black and blue and scabbed over. At the start of class, I went to my PE teacher, Ms. L, and asked if I could be excused from dressing out until the bruises cleared up. When I showed her, she gasped and covered her mouth.

"Who did this to you?" she firmly asked.

"My parents. But mostly my stepmom."

Ms. L stood up from inspecting my legs, put her hands on her hips, and turned away from me. She took a few deep breaths. Then she put her hands on her head, shook her head no, and turned back around to me.

"OK, you're excused from dressing out for 2 weeks," she said. "We'll look at it again then," and she quickly left her office.

***

To my knowledge, nothing happened as a result of showing my PE teacher. I mean, there were no meetings with Child Protective Services (CPS), or the school Principal. My parents didn't say anything to me either, so I guess no one contacted them from the school or the county.

When my bruises started clearing up, I dressed out and wore sweats.

THE ANNOUNCEMENT

"Karlin, we're sending you to a boarding school!" Sandy announced.

"What?" I exclaimed.

"What? ... What??" Ellen and Lulu chimed in.

"What, what, what?" Sandy mocked. "Yep! We're sending you to French Camp Academy."

"What? Where??" I looked at Daddy incredulously. But Sandy did all the talking.

"Pack your bags! Bye-bye!" She laughed.

She was the only one laughing. *There's that get-rid-of-Karlin theme again. Maybe something really is wrong with me?*

Sandy got serious and explained, "It's a Christian boarding school. You'll go to school there and live in a dorm and come home on the holidays. It'll be like college, kind of."

I searched Daddy's eyes. "You want to … send me away?" I choked.

Dad answered me, but Sandy kept talking. I didn't hear a word either of them said. I looked around the living room, trying to slow down my racing thoughts so I could attempt to make sense of what just exploded in my world. I looked at my sisters sitting on the couch. Ellen's eyebrows were furled; she was mad. Little Lulu had the widest eyes, full of tears waiting to flow down her cheeks. I looked down at the floor and blinked hard. A tear fell on my foot.

"Karlin, are you listening to us?" Sandy nagged.

I looked at Dad and Sandy intently. Dad's green eyes were sad and apprehensive. He knew there would be pushback. Sandy grinned with such smugness. This was her idea.

"No," I said low and firm.

"What?!?" Sandy was indignant.

Daddy closed his eyes for a long pause.

"I heard you. But I'm not going." I said as matter-of-factly as possible.

Whatever this was, the conflict between Sandy and me had just escalated to DEFCON 1. I was fighting this openly—no tricks, no mind games, no secret moves. I was so determined, like a tick dug in. This was war. And Daddy was collateral damage.

For days and weeks that turned into months, I fought with Dad and Sandy about going away to this French whatever school. I screamed and cried in protest and threw unsightly fits. But I also reasoned with precise intent.

"Mom just died 11 months ago, Dad. I'm not ready to be separated from my sisters right now. I can't live without them. I would miss them so much." I stabbed with these last two lines over and over again.

"...What about me, Peanut? Won't you miss me, too?" Daddy kept meekly asking.

I wouldn't answer.

Sandy could whip me ten more times; I wasn't leaving my sisters.

After what felt like three months of turmoil, the subject faded away. Dad and Sandy never brought it up again. I don't want to flex my muscles or claim victory, because I never intended to hurt my dad like that, or in any way. But maybe my message was clear: Karlin can't be separated from her sisters right now. It would be too traumatic for all three of them.

HANDBOOK

One late afternoon in the spring of my eighth-grade year, I was cleaning out my bedroom desk. I came across the Student Guide and Handbook of French Camp Academy (FCA). I didn't realize I even had it.

I flopped onto my bed and opened it.

"Let's see what kind of medieval rules these are," I scoffed. – Yikes! I was right.

Everything — from the dress code, makeup policy, dating rules, telephone contact with parents, grades, work details, and dormitories to discipline that included paddling — was strict, old-fashioned, and very "religious." It sounded very dull, very regimented, and very boring. Who would want to go to this school? Who would want to leave the world for this sheltered bubble? What happy teenage—

I paused. My thoughts were flying, but not due to chaos and confusion or emotional trauma. They were soaring and gliding. No fear, no anger. Just ... serenity.

Wait, wait, wait! STOP! ...What about my sisters? *They'll be fine if it's what you want. It's you she loathes.*

But I fought so hard to stay. I hurt my dad's heart in the process. *He'll be ok if it's what you want. There will be some peace for your dad and in the home if you go. And that's what everyone needs right now. Peace.*

I sat up and dried my eyes. I took a deep breath. Is this what I really want? *Yes. You all need this. Everything will work out for the good.*

I exhaled. "Ok then..."

I knocked on Daddy's bedroom door. Lying in bed watching TV, he turned the doorknob, and the door swung open.

"Hey, Peanut!" he said cheerfully.

I held onto the doorway and leaned in like a monkey until I saw his face. "Daddy? I've been thinking… I think I'd like to try this French Camp thing. I think it could be a good thing."

Daddy sat up. "But Peanut, I thought you were firm about staying with your sisters?"

"I know I was… and I'm sorry," I said, trying not to cry.

"Well, Peanut, I'm not so sure I want you to go myself," he admitted.

"I'll come home on holidays and breaks, and once a month. We can call each other once a week, Daddy. I don't think it will be as bad as I thought."

Daddy rubbed his eyes. "Are you sure, Peanut? Is this really what you want?"

"I think I'm pretty sure…" and I paused. "Daddy, I believe this will be good for me, and good for the whole family. The family needs peace, and I think that'll only happen if I leave."

Daddy rubbed his eyes some more. "Alright then. I'll arrange an interview and a campus tour."

"Thank you, Daddy." I hugged my hero.

"We don't want you here if you don't want to be here."

He sat behind his wooden executive desk, leaning forward over his clasped hands, his stern gaze fixed on me. He squinted his eyes as if he were sifting through my secrets. Like the time Ellen helped me sneak out of our bedroom window. I never did it again, but Daddy never knew.

Ralph Newman was the Dean of Students at French Camp Academy, with a permanent scowl, and someone I wouldn't want to cross. "Do you understand me, Karlin?"

"Yes, sir. I do want to be here." I said with wide eyes.
Blink, blink, blink.

"Great. We'll see you back here this summer then." He got up and went to talk privately with my parents, patting my head as he walked by.

It was spring break, 3 months until my life would drastically change. Again.

A ROCK AND A HARD SPOT

It was a tough day near the end of 8th grade. Sandy and I were relentless with each other as she took her bitterness out on Ellen and Lulu as well. Daddy brought me inside to talk with him.

"Peanut, I don't know what else to do. This has got to stop." He reasoned.

"Tell HER to stop!" I countered. "Daddy, it's like she's trying to pick a fight with me on purpose, all the time! She keeps calling me vain, saying that I can't walk past a reflective surface without looking at myself. So what?!? Who cares? Why does she keep needling me about this? She picks on me!"

Dad took a contemplative breath. "I know that your mom's passing away and having to come live with us hasn't been easy for you girls. But Sandy is struggling too. She's never been a mom before, and all of a sudden, three girls just dropped into her lap."

I heard what Daddy said. And I realized how all of this might be tough for Sandy, too. But I couldn't appreciate any of it.

"Daddy, it's more than just 'hard on Sandy, too'. I know she hates me. It's like she's punishing us, especially me, for being here."

"She doesn't hate you, Peanut."

"Dad!" I begged. "She told us last year that she doesn't love us. And I believe her! Nothing about her actions shows 'I care about you'. She's so mean to us, Daddy. And you don't do anything about it." – This was my wise, mature self speaking. And to this day, I'm still amazed at how well I expressed that at 14 years old.

Daddy's face turned so sad, and his eyes got red. "I'm between a rock and a hard spot, Peanut."
What does that mean?

And just like that, I was a box of rocks again.

Then he began to cry. "I love my wife … and I love my daughters so very much. I want all of you to love each other and get along, but I don't know how to make that happen."

All my pride, stubbornness, and rebellion melted away as I witnessed my dad's vulnerability. It ached my heart.

"If I confront Sandy, she gets mad at me," he continued. "If I get on to you, then you get mad at me. I just can't win."

"I'm sorry, Daddy," I choked in a whisper. "I think it's kinda normal for teens to get angry at their parents, but you and your wife shouldn't be fighting about me." *Whoa! There I go again with some mind-blowing wisdom. Where did that come from?*

"I know I haven't made things easy," I admitted. "But I'll work on it. But why, Daddy? Why does Sandy hate me? I was actually looking forward to her being our mom. So I know it wasn't me who started all this."

"No, it wasn't you, Peanut," Daddy said, wiping his eyes. "Sandy struggles with self-esteem issues; she's very jealous and insecure. It used to just be her and me. Now, she has to share me with all of you. She's not used to that. Instead of raising her own children from infancy, she's now got three half-grown girls. She's never done this before; she doesn't know what to do."

I listened. I thought deeply about his words.

"I can only imagine how rough this is for Sandy as well," I empathized. "But WHY is she so cruel? WHY does she go out of her way to start fights with me?"

I was begging for answers.

"Well, Peanut," Daddy sighed. "Part of Sandy's insecurities is that you look like your mother."

I paused and blinked several times.

"Dad— Mom's dead," I said with a hint of condescension. "There's no competition. The threat's gone. I can't help that I look like her. Does this mean she's going to keep picking on me?"

"No, no, no, Peanut. Of course not."

"Well, if that's the only way she knows how to treat me– because I look like my dead mom," I concluded, "maybe it is a good thing that I'm going away to French Camp."

I didn't believe Sandy would eventually stop picking on me. Daddy was just being hopeful, and I couldn't blame him for that. He also hadn't done much to intervene on my behalf because he didn't like confrontations, so I had no reason to believe him. But I hoped right alongside him anyway, from a distance.

I sure loved him.

***

Sandy was 30, just 16 years older than me. Old enough to know better in every way, on every level. So, I didn't cut her any slack; I didn't accept her inexperience as an excuse to be a bully. Even her insecurities didn't justify her meanness. Being cruel is not an oopsie. It's very intentional. Sandy could have failed Stepparenting 101, and no one would have cared if she were simply nice. Even if she had never been a parent and had no clue, just be nice! It would have been the right thing to do.

CHAPTER 8
French Camp Academy

Daddy stuffed my last suitcase into the small red VW trunk, and I hugged my sisters goodbye. Actually, I hugged Lulu. Ellen just punched me. It was a warm, sunny June day in 1980.

Located on the beautiful Natchez Trace Parkway at mile marker 180 was the historical French Camp Academy, a Christ-centered school home.

The campus hustled and bustled with new dorm students' registration and returning students unpacking after their summer break at home. I observed my surroundings attentively, taking special note of the students' interactions with each other and the staff. I could tell who was popular. I spotted the brainiacs and the nerds. I recognized the athletes. And I identified the extroverts, the introverts, the confident, the low self-esteem, the well-off, and the poor. The poor were easy to find. They looked like me, wearing nothing trendy or fashionable, just faded and worn. But I think I was the only one still wearing corduroy bell bottoms – a California thing, I think. Where would I fit in? Where could I insert myself?

Dad and Sandy helped me carry my suitcases to Griffin Dorm, and we met my dorm parents, Mr. and Mrs. Ainsworth. The adults talked for a few minutes, sharing information. I was informed that I'd be getting a roommate by the end of the week. *Oh wow! This really does feel college-like.*

I hugged Daddy goodbye, long and tight. He kissed the top of my head and winked, "Be good, Peanut." His eyes were a little red and shiny, which made his green eyes stand out and sparkle.

I hugged Sandy with one of those arms-wide-open, barely-touching pat, pat, pat hugs. Then she gave me one of those wiggly finger waves

close to her face with a snarky giggle, "Toodaloo! … Byyyyye!"
Bye Witch!

I stood under a giant oak tree and watched them drive away until they turned left and out of sight.

There I was, by myself, all alone without my family. And it was … exciting, in a new beginning kind of way. I was alone, but I didn't feel alone— and I hadn't even made any friends yet.

I ran back to my dorm. I stood where the linoleum and carpet met and looked down.

We'd been living in trailer parks in Mississippi. When my sisters and I first arrived, we lived in a 2-bedroom sardine-can trailer in a mobile home park. Then Daddy moved us into a 3-bedroom trailer in a homely park that gave new meaning to trailer park trash. We were so poor. I guess the US Navy didn't pay very well back then? But surely our mom's survivor benefits made up for some of it? The old carpet at home was matted, lacked padding, and was gross and hard.

I took my shoes off and stepped onto the dorm's carpet. I curled my toes on the shag rug and took a deep breath, closing my eyes. This was my heaven. *Thank you, God!*

SANCTUARY

I got into the groove of this private, tiny Christian school home. It wasn't hard at all for me to adapt. As a matter of fact, I had to be reminded to write to my dad on the weekends and call home. I had a roommate and dorm mates who became my friends. Other than the dorm parents living in their attached apartment at the other end of the dorm, I did feel a little grown up. Sure, the rules were stringent, but we all broke them to some extent from time to time. Just like we all did at home. Sometimes we were restricted to the dorm, sometimes to our rooms, sometimes we got "dating restriction" for kissing our boyfriend, and occasionally, we got paddled. – All of which we deserved for breaking the rules, whether we admitted it or not.

Some students felt they were being jailed by their parents' decisions and did not want to be there. I felt free, liberated, and at home.

I found my sanctuary.

MY MASK

For Independence Day, I went home for the holiday and the long weekend.

While I was away, the family had been busy moving into 3752 York Rd in Lauderdale, an 80-year-old house that Dad and Sandy wanted to restore to its 1900 era. I joined Ellen and Lulu in pulling up layers of old linoleum – not by choice, of course – revealing the house's original wood floors. Even though I'd been away 6 weeks and was now officially living at the school, the 3 of us still bickered as if I'd never left.

I came home wearing makeup. Makeup that my new friends gave me. As expected, Sandy criticized and ridiculed me. Daddy didn't say anything. He must have thrown his hands up, picking his battles.

Yes, I was wrong to disobey. But stronger than my conviction of disobedience was my low self-esteem and a self-diagnosed inferiority complex. I felt pretty when I wore makeup. It was also my mask. I hid my deep hurts behind it. If I looked pretty, I felt pretty. If I felt pretty, I was extroverted, confident, and happy-go-lucky … on the outside. I needed my mask like the Phantom of the Opera needed his. And I disobeyed my parents for that.

14 years old, dead mom, wicked stepmother, passive dad, new boarding school – I felt like a newborn foal wobbling on its legs. Mom had been gone for 18 months now. That was still fresh. That wound was deep. And whatever healing was happening, it wasn't visible on the surface. I'm not even sure I felt like I was healing at all. Not once did Sandy ask how my sisters and I were doing emotionally and mentally after such a traumatic loss. Instead, she was cruel.

After the 4th of July, I went back to French Camp.

Ellen and Lulu grumbled during yardwork.

"Hey! … There will be none of that!" Daddy warned. "Quit your griping, or I'll tan your hide and give you something to gripe about."

I don't know if that was just a standard parental threat or if Daddy really intended to paddle them.

Ellen muttered, but loud enough for Dad to hear. "I remember what you and Sandy did to Karlin's legs. If you touch us, I'll call the police."

And I don't know if Ellen really intended to do that either. But Daddy looked away.

FRESHMAN

Summer ended, and school started. I was in 9th grade.

Unlike most students, I did not begin the new school year in high school with new clothes, and I felt so embarrassed. Partly because that's what I was used to with Mom, and mainly because I saw that everyone else around me was used to that as well.

I hid my embarrassment behind a fake smile and a bubbly, perky attitude of 'my-old-clothes-are-just-fine,' trying not to think about it. This was when my mask was most effective.

I tried out for cheerleading and was selected! I signed up for the chorus and sang glorious music of praise and worship to the Lord across the state. I made honor roll that semester! Oh, and I had a boyfriend who was a senior and the football team captain. Was I finally healing? If so, I'll take it!

THANKSGIVING

I went home to Lauderdale for Thanksgiving and the long weekend.

I remember it feeling somewhat peaceful. Perhaps because Sandy was busy in the kitchen, focused on cooking. I don't know where Daddy went in the morning, but he rushed in through the front door dirty, disheveled, and wide-eyed.

"Sandy! I just flipped the truck!" he yelled.

She met Daddy in the hallway, "WHAT?!? … Oh my god, Jim, are you ok???"

Then my sisters and I came running out of our bedroom full of questions and concern.

"Girls, girls, I'm ok," Daddy assured us.

A deer ran out in front of his truck, and he turned hard to miss it. The truck flipped and slid on the top of the cab for about 100 yards, he said. The cab was crunched in, but he was able to crawl out through the shattered rear windshield.

"Jim, you'd better be careful! … This could be a sign!" Sandy warned. *A sign of what?*

"Oh, don't be silly. I'm ok!" Daddy quipped.

Later that afternoon, as Dad was working on Sandy's car, showing Ellen what spark plugs were, she asked him, "Dad? Do you believe in God?"

"Monster, I pray every night for you girls. Don't you worry about God and me."

CHRISTMAS

I went back home for Christmas break.

It was the same situation between Sandy and me, but this time with Christmas decorations. I was happy to see my sisters, but it didn't change how much we bickered. Sisters will be sisters.

At FCA, we lived the church life and received religious instruction. Church every Sunday morning and evening; Devotions at breakfast and supper every day; Chapel every Monday through Friday between 2nd and 3rd period; Wednesday night vespers; Bible classes for academic requirements; and more devotions in our dorms. Jesus was crammed down our throats, literally. I hated going to church.

Wait. Let me rephrase that. I hated being *forced* to go to church. I just hated waking up, getting dressed, and going. I wanted to sleep in more than just on Saturday mornings, which meant forfeiting breakfast.

But, oddly as it may seem, and, as it turned out, while visiting home, I got up and went to church on my own accord. I called the church and arranged my own transportation. And I didn't mind one bit.

With all the Jesus cramming, I remembered Hebrews 12:11.

> "No discipline seems pleasant at the time, but painful. Later on, however, it produces a harvest of righteousness and peace for those who have been trained by it."

HUNTING

"Come on. Let's go hunting," Daddy said.

"OK!" I said excitedly. It was always a treat to go hunting with Daddy.

"Hold on!" I added and ran to the bathroom. "I'll be right out!"

"Hurry up, Peanut. We're burning daylight." John Wayne used to say that in his movie, The Cowboys.

I didn't have to tinkle, so I didn't close the bathroom door all the way. But Ellen came along and flung the door open.

"What are you doing?!?" She said with irritation.

"Can I have some privacy, please???" I tried shoving her out of the bathroom.

"OH MY GOSH! ARE YOU PUTTING ON MAKEUP TO GO HUNTING?!?" *Could you yell it any louder?*

"I'm just freshening up! GET OUT!" I justified, stupidly.

"FOR WHAT?!? THE ANIMALS?!? … YOU'RE SO STUPID!!!" Ellen laughed incredulously.

And of course, Sandy heard and came out of the kitchen to add her insults. *I hate everyone!*

Daddy and I got out of the truck and hiked into the woods. The sky was overcast behind him as I looked up at him, listening carefully to what he was teaching me about nature. His breath was visible in the cold, and his handsome green-eyed face looked so peaceful.

We reached a small creek, and Daddy crossed it. I usually followed right behind him, never thinking twice. But I stopped... because... I didn't want to get my shoes wet. And what if I tripped and slid, messed up my makeup, and got dirty?

When Daddy noticed I wasn't behind him, he stopped and saw me still standing on the other side.

"C'mon, Peanut, what are you waiting for?"

"Daddy, I—I can't. I might fall."

I'll never forget the look on his face. It was both disappointment and the realization that his eldest princess had just arrived.

Daddy came back for me and carried me across that little creek.

ELLEN'S TURN

Since Sandy no longer had me to pick on, her focus shifted to Ellen, and their clashes grew more frequent.

Apparently, Jim's daughters were such troublemakers that Sandy convinced Daddy to send another one away. Ellen didn't want to leave, but she didn't protest either.

After the Christmas break, Ellen came back to French Camp with me. She was in Heidelberg dorm.

FIRST HEARTBREAK

Shortly after the second semester started, my senior football team captain boyfriend broke up with me. My first real boyfriend.

I was heartbroken. I sneaked back to my dorm after lunch without permission and cried as hard as I could in my bathroom. I let it all out, and no one knew except God.

When I ran out of tears, I pulled myself together, fixed my makeup, and collected my thoughts. I walked out of the dorm and headed back to the school building with my head held high.

I was broken inside, but no one ever knew it… except God and me.

SUMMERTIME

My freshman year and Ellen's junior high year ended. I was 15, Ellen was 14, and we went home to Lauderdale for the summer.

Daddy was always big on hugs and pinches on the nose. But Sandy? Not so much. I watched her closely and could tell she wasn't thrilled about our return for the summer. She didn't make eye contact and gave short answers, as if she was shy or talking to strangers. But Daddy was either oblivious, playing it down, didn't care, or all of the above.

Dad and Sandy now had a garden we needed to tend. By then, I was full-on foofoo frilly. Working in the dirt was just ridiculous and so gross that I threw a little hissy fit.

"Just shut up and do it!" Ellen growled at me as she got on all four to pull weeds.

"I wouldn't ask you to do something I wouldn't do or haven't done myself, Peanut," Daddy said encouragingly. *Pfft! What does that even mean?*

GRASS & CREEPY CRAWLIES

Ellen usually mowed the big lawn, but on this particular day—I can't remember where she was—I was voluntold to do it. Lulu was probably on the back porch hanging out with the horde of cats we had, or tucked away somewhere reading a book.

I put up a fuss, of course. And of course, I lost. But if I had to mow this huge yard by myself, I was determined to get something out of it. So, I threw on a tank top and shorts and slathered myself with Hawaiian Blend dark tanning oil.

Dad and Sandy sat on the front porch and watched my glistening self walk down the steps as if it were the red carpet, leaving an invisible trail of tropical coconut in my wake.

Daddy chuckled.

Sandy barked, "You know you're going to get grass all over you, don't you?"

"Maybe. Maybe not," I smugged, rolling my eyes.

I flung my hair back as a show of *go-ahead-and-laugh-I-don't-care*, but my dark strands got tangled around my oily fingers.

Daddy chuckled again.

"God, you're so vain, Karlin!" Sandy laughed. *Yes, yes, you keep telling me this.*

I had some trouble starting the lawnmower. I didn't realize I needed to lift weights and build muscle for it. So Daddy came off the porch and gave me some pointers.

"Slide this up… hold this down… pull this hard… do it again if it doesn't start… when it starts, slide this back… see that clump of grass? Be careful, it's a tree stump."

"Ummm… OK."

Daddy took another look at my shiny arms and shook his head, chuckling as he walked back to the porch.

I rolled my eyes. *Whatever.*

I got the mower started—after nearly dislocating my shoulder (well, that's what it felt like!)—and began pushing down the first row.

Wait! There's no bag! WHERE'S THE GRASS BAG?!?

With one hand on the bar to keep the mower on, I turned to my parents, still sitting on the porch, and raised my other hand in question. Sandy raised both her hands back at me, shaking her head "no" with a crazed grin, and mouthed, "There is no bag," then doubled over laughing maniacally. I'm so glad I couldn't hear her. Daddy dropped his head, but I could see his shoulders shaking, so I knew he was laughing too. I spat out the grass and twigs that stuck to my lip gloss with my free hand. Then I switched hands on the bar and used my other hand to pick the same stuff out of my mascaraed eyelashes. *UUUUGH!*

I pushed on, mowing, throwing a silent nuclear temper tantrum.

Three-quarters of the way through, I couldn't take it anymore. I stopped the mower and looked down at my legs. Then at my arms. I was covered—no, *coated*—with grass clippings. Then I scratched an itch on my forehead, and my face was caked with grass and whatever little creepy bugs were crawling around in it. I looked like the Jolly Green midget!

I turned to march back to the house... and my parents were laughing even harder and louder. Daddy didn't even bother to hide it anymore.

Now I stomped back to the house and trudged up the stairs to the porch.

"Can I take a bath, please?!?" My voice cracked with frustration.

"Yes, Peanut," he said softly, obviously trying not to laugh. "Take a bath. You can finish the rest tomorrow."

I stomped inside the house and let the screen door slam shut behind me.

My parents fell out laughing again.

THE WILL

One evening, Daddy and I were sitting on the front porch swing, enjoying the sunset.

"Peanut, Sandy, and I made our wills." He said. "By the time you and your sisters reach 21, you're going to have so much money in your trust from your Mom's estate."

"Really? How much?"

"Over a hundred thousand dollars. That's more money than I'll ever see."

"Oh wow!" I really didn't know what else to say.

I honestly didn't understand what all of that really meant. I didn't realize how much 100K meant in the context of the early 1980s economic climate. I barely understood the estate and trust fund stuff.

"So, Sandy and I made your cousins Nicole and Jenny, and Linda and Cy our heirs." Daddy continued. "If something ever happens to us, your cousins will get everything."

"… Ok," I said softly and shrugged.

I mean, Dad and Sandy didn't have much. Even by Mississippi's standards, which was the poorest state in the union, we were still pretty broke. It's not like we were missing out on some multimillion-dollar estate. So I was indifferent, at least as a 15-year-old. That kind of stuff just wasn't important to me. I had other pressing issues to worry about as I entered the 10th grade—like my cute boyfriend, cheerleader tryouts, and makeup.

However, what mattered to me was that Daddy's own children wouldn't be his heirs when he died. Even if penniless, I believe any child would prefer to receive nothing rather than be cut out of a will as if they never existed. And then to be replaced by other children who weren't their own.

They had their wills drawn up 18 months before Daddy told me this. Was he waiting for the right moment?

I will go to my grave convinced that this was another one of Sandy's ideas.

***

French Camp Academy is still in operation today. And it remains a sanctuary for many deserving young teens, providing love and stability while teaching the Gospel through an exemplary academic curriculum.

CHAPTER 9
Ellen

Ellen Elizabeth — Oh, I'm sorry. I meant MONSTER– was a bruiser. I didn't exaggerate when I said she was the brother Lulu and I never had. Daddy called her Monster, but Lulu and I had another name for her: Big Bad John.

Shortly after moving to the States, I remember our first Christmas when Mom gave us the leftover garland to play with. I found one of Daddy's Johnny Cash records and played our favorite song, Big Bad John. Lulu and I wrapped ourselves in the silver garland and wrestled Ellen, two against one. She kicked our skinny butts every single time.

She was a snatcher, too. Anytime there were gifts that we were given a choice of, Ellen always got first pick. Always. Because she would snatch what she wanted, "That's mine!"

One evening, Ellen and I answered the door to a salesman. While Ellen went to get Mom, he handed me two lollipops and said, "Here you go. And give this one to your brother."

"I don't have a brother. That's my little sister. But, thank you."

When I gave Ellen her sucker, I scolded, "You need to wear your earrings! You look like a boy!"

"So?" and she punched me.

ADRENALINE

Shortly after moving to Mississippi, Ellen kept getting teased by a few girls in her 6th-grade class.

With no mother, a new school, and a whole new culture in a different state, Ellen was very quiet and kept to herself.

One day, in the library, that handful of girls sent another girl to Ellen's table to show her a picture of a bunch of dogs in an encyclopedia.

"You see that one?" she said to Ellen, pointing to a dog. "That's you."

Ellen jumped up, flung the book out of her face, shoved the girl against the wall, and started punching her.

School staff broke up the fight, but the teachers were afraid to send Ellen back to class because she was still so mad.

Back at home, it was quiet around the dinner table until Daddy broke the silence.

"So, Monster?" he asked gently. "I heard you got expelled from school today?"

"Yes, I did, Daddy," she quietly said.

Before putting a spoonful of food in his mouth, he asked, "Why did you fight her, Monster?"

Ellen shrugged and said, "I dunno. I guess my adrenaline was pumping. But I'm not taking that crap anymore!"

Daddy hunched his back, covered his mouth, and tried not to choke on his chili. He was not expecting that answer.

When he finally swallowed, he laughed.

"Well, the next time that happens, you need to do this..." and Daddy continued to give his Monster all the pointers she needed to defend herself if she had to again.

But no one picked on her after that.

Ellen was also the sister who, when I asked, "You wouldn't hit someone with glasses, would you?" punched me in the gut instead.

CHAPTER 10
Little Lulu

She's 3 ½ years younger than me, but I don't remember life without Lulu. I don't remember seeing Mom pregnant, but I do remember watching Mom try to breastfeed her. Lulu was tiny—she must have been only a few weeks old.

I also remember our housegirl letting me change Lulu's diaper when she was a few months old— I accidentally safety-pinned it through her skin! OUCH! I must have been acting like a brat for our housegirl to let me try that at 4 years old.

Lulu was just 9 years old when Mom died, and her world was turned upside down. I can't say that time healed anything or that life became easier for her, but she found ways to cope in an environment she couldn't escape.

With Ellen and me gone, there were no more fights. No one paid attention to Lulu, which she loved! She was only 12 but didn't have to answer to anyone. She was free! So, in that sense, that was a good time for Lulu. She was overlooked, but there was peace.

She spent whole days outside, barefoot, traipsing around in the woods near an old swimming hole, fishing and pretending she was Karana from the book, Island of the Blue Dolphins. She could be seen catching crawdads in ditches and turning over rocks to find worms for bait.

Daddy's only rule for her was to take a dog everywhere she went. Later, her personal dog and companion, Big Red, often stood between her and a sudden attack by a crazed rooster…

I was out playing in the yard one day when that damn rooster charged at me. I was way out in the side yard with no 'weapon' (meaning a broom!) nearby. So I took off running. I was so small and scrawny, and I swear that rooster was half my size! Anyway, I ran as fast as I could. I must have stepped on uneven ground or tripped over something unseen, because I went down. And that damn rooster wasted NO time jumping on my head. I tried to get up, but that frikken bird was determined to end my life! He was in my hair, squawking and doing his best to claw my eyes out. There was no escaping that demon bird. With my last breath, I let out the loudest scream I could muster. I tried to curl up and cover my face, accepting my end, when I heard da-domp, da-domp, DA-DOMP. I dared a glance up just in time to see Big Red giving chase. He trotted back toward me, and I just threw my arms around him and hugged him. He literally saved my life!

– Lulu

When she wasn't reading, she was bike riding, exploring by herself.

Sometime after Big Red went missing, Lulu found an old, old cemetery while riding down a dirt trail leading into a wooded area. She used to pack a lunch—a hot dog wrapped in a slice of white bread with ketchup—and go on a picnic by herself at the cemetery. And sometimes she brought a book, Little House on the Prairie. She would read for hours, all alone, but not at all afraid.

She was a dirty little poor Mississippi woods girl, always pulling ticks off of herself.

When Lulu joined the Little League team, Daddy went to all her games. He was so proud of his Wow.

When Dad and Sandy went out to dinner, though, they left her alone at home at night, and that's what terrified her.

And Sandy even sent Lulu to work in her antique shop all by herself when she was only 11 years old.

One time, Lulu told Daddy that she was bored, so he handed her a Reader's Digest. She fell in love with them.

When she wasn't on her lonesome adventures in the woods, she went fishing with Daddy every chance she could get; everything possible to stay invisible and fly under Sandy's radar.

Lulu was mostly left to her own devices. For example, no one questioned her when she burned an entire box of matches (500 count, to be exact) – a few at a time – in her bedroom.

Or when she asked Daddy for some wood glue, he simply handed it to her without any questions. But the pride in his eyes when she showed him a matchstick house was priceless! And as Daddy would say, "Wow!"

Neglected, dirty, self-entertained, resourceful, and exploited by child labor, Lulu was 100% Generation X.

As a matter of fact, Daddy told her, "Hey, Wow, if you gotta use the bathroom in the woods, just dig yourself a little hole." And SHE DID! My baby sister had no qualms pooping in the woods by herself!

Lulu put the feral in Gen X!

CHAPTER 11
Shredded

We used to have a washer and dryer. In 1981, who didn't?

Oh, just a family who bought a Turn-of-the-Century home to restore it to its original era and then live *it* as well. So Dad and Sandy got rid of the modern appliances – because they didn't have Maytags, Whirlpools, and Speed Queens in 1900 - and we had to use a metal tub and washboard and hang our clothes on the line to dry… or take our laundry to the local convenience store/gas station/laundromat. We chose the latter.

Ellen and I were in 9th and 10th grade at French Camp Academy, so little Lulu was left to do the laundry. One weekend, she had a friend over, and Dad and Sandy decided it was laundry day. Lulu was so embarrassed that she had to ask her friend for help.

The laundromat was just a short walk around the corner from the house, so Dad dropped them off in the late afternoon and either headed back home to work on renovation projects or hung out at the convenience store, having a beer and being neighborly to everyone. In such a deep southern podunk town, I don't think anyone cared about public drinking or loitering. Dad found one of his shirts on the ground that had fallen out of the basket, so he went back to the laundromat and tossed it to Lulu. Lulu mumbled under her breath, "I hate you."

Several hours later, way past dark, Sandy answered the phone. "Hello?"

"Um, can you pick us up?" Lulu asked from the pay phone. "We've been done for a while."

"What? Where's your dad?"

"I dunno."

Sandy paused. "…Ok. Give me a minute."

A whole 6 minutes later, back at the house, Sandy pulled dinner out of the oven and served Lulu and Felicity. Lulu took three bites of her mashed potatoes when they all heard the sirens.

Hearing sirens at various times of the day in any large city is standard. No one thinks twice about them. But in Lauderdale, Mississippi, especially on a Sunday night, it was uncommon.

Sandy grabbed her car keys and ran out of the house, "I have to follow that!"

Lulu lost her appetite.

Time passed. But how can you measure eternity?

Sandy came home alone.

"Lulu … I need to talk to you."

Sandy followed the lights and sirens from her red 1972 VW Beetle.

Up a few miles on northbound Hwy 45, Sandy stopped in front of a small crowd of police, paramedics, looky-loos, and stopped traffic on the highway.

"What's going on?" she asked the constable.

"Oh, there's some dead man in the middle of the road."

Sandy broke through the crowd and ran towards the body silhouetted by vehicle headlights.

"JIM???" she cried and crumbled to her knees.

She crawled the rest of the way to her husband, wailing, yelling his name. Her thick, long mane of wavy chestnut brown hair separated her and my dad from the rest of the world as she hovered over him, begging, "Don't leave me, Jim! Please don't leave me..."

The crowd watched.

She wailed again at the stars of the deep blue night sky, from the deepest, most broken part of her heart, "NOOOOOOOOOOOO, nooooooo don't leave me, Jim! … JIM! … Please, PLEASE don't leave me."

Sandy sobbed over my dad's face, her tears dropping on him, mixing with his blood coming from his nose and mouth. She lifted her head enough to see his broken bones protruding from his shirt. Her assessment continued to his legs and socked feet. Sandy looked around on the road. One of Daddy's boots was on the side of the road. The other was never found.

"Oh, Jim," Sandy cried.

Sandy's tears continued to rain over Daddy's face as she sat on the road, hovering over his head in her lap. Time stood still. This was a nightmare she will never wake up from.

Certainty had set in now, and she finally lifted her head. She brushed her tear-drenched hair back, wiped her face off with her hands, and wiped them dry on her jeans.

She whispered, "I love you," to her husband, laid his head gently on the ground, and stood up. She flung her hair back over her shoulders and steeled herself.

Sandy walked back towards the crowd as the paramedics moved in with their gurney. Headlights blinded her. All eyes were locked on her as they all realized they had just witnessed something unthinkable.

Sandy walked up to the constable, grabbed him by the shirt, and shoved him against his car.

"That dead man … is MY HUSBAND!" she yelled.

Sandy's life would never be the same.

AT THE OFFICE

Lulu's friend called her mother to come pick her up.

"NO! NO! NO!" 12-year-old Lulu protested.
"Not again!" She thought over and over.
"Not Daddy, too!" she cried.

When Felicity's mother arrived, she offered to take Lulu with her. Lulu refused to go; she wanted to be with Sandy. But Sandy insisted.

Felicity went to school the next day, but Lulu went to work with Ms. Adams. As she sat in a chair near Ms. Adams's desk all day, doing absolutely nothing but thinking, thinking, thinking, the news came on the radio in the office.

> *One man dead in a pedestrian vs motor vehicle accident on North Hwy 45 near the Lauderdale/Kemper county line last night. Jim Davis, a resident of Lauderdale …*

Ms. Adams looked at Lulu as she was looking down, fidgeting with her hands in her lap.

Ms. Adams got up from her desk, went to Lulu, and held her. Just held her.

AGAIN

My after-school work detail at FCA was the craft shop, when I wasn't at cheerleader practice or running track.

In the craft shop, we quilted, crocheted, knitted, embroidered, cross-stitched, and created all kinds of arts and crafts to sell at the French Camp Visitors' Center, supporting the school's ministry to its students.

While sitting around the quilt, chatting with my fellow schoolmates as Mrs. Johnson, our work supervisor, kept reminding us to get back to work, my dorm parent, Mr. Ainsworth, came in. He spoke quietly with Mrs. Johnson, then called my name.

Mr. Ainsworth was a deep-voiced, soft-spoken, serious man who, to me, resembled Clint Eastwood! He was the ultimate bad-boy greaser during '50s Day dress-up on campus.

Mr. Ainsworth never came into the craft shop; he had his own work crew to supervise. So naturally I said, "Hey?!?"

"Karlin, you need to come with me, please," he said in his usual, serious tone, but turned up a notch.

"What's wrong? Am I in trouble?"

"No. But we need to go back to the dorm."

I jumped into his work van and asked a few more questions. "Mr. Ainsworth, what's going on??"

"Karlin? Please. Just wait until we get to the dorm, ok?"

"Yes, sir."

My memory is like a dream sometimes. Sometimes blurry, sometimes so vivid. I don't know how people show up in my dreams sometimes, but *POOF* there they are.

POOF Ellen was waiting around at my dorm. As I was going through the main floor sliding glass door, I wondered why Ellen was even there at all, especially during work detail.

"Karlin? Ellen? Come on in." Mr. Ainsworth ushered us into his apartment.

As he opened the door, we could see Sandy sitting on their couch, with Mrs. Ainsworth next to her.

Ellen walked in first and, by reflex, said, "Oh, hi, Daddy!"

But when I walked in, I stopped and looked around, trying to figure out why we were brought here. What kind of an inquisition was this? But I didn't see Daddy.

"Karlin and Ellen? Come sit down," Sandy said.

I sat next to Sandy and noticed that her hair was in a low pony and the rims of her eyes were red. She had been crying. And now I was hearing a crack in her voice.

Ellen asked, "Where's Dad?

"What's wrong?" I insisted.

Sandy took a deep breath. "Last night … your dad was helping a truck driver who had broken down on the side of the road. As your dad was walking across the highway back to his truck, he was hit by a drunk driver …"

"What?!?" Ellen yelled incredulously.

"Oh no!" I exclaimed, "Is he going to be alright?"

Sandy sniffled, dropped her head, and started crying. My eyes searched her intensely. I looked around the room for answers, and all the staff members present—Ellen's dorm parents, mine, the school president, and a few others I can't recall—were either looking down or at the ceiling. Except Ellen's dorm mother. She was staring at Ellen with tear-filled eyes, longing to go to her. Tears were streaming down Mrs. Ainsworth's cheeks as she looked at me with wide eyes. A familiar dread was beginning to creep over me.

"He didn't make it," Sandy cried. "Your dad died."

"NOOOOOOOOOOOOOOOOOOOOOOOOOOOO!"
I screamed as loud as I could for as long as my breath would let me. I wailed from the core of all that was me. My universe was now completely shredded apart; 15 years old, no mom, no dad.

I fell to the floor and screamed some more, grabbing the carpet as if trying to shred it apart, the way life was shredding me. I cried and cried, wailed and cried, "Please God, nooooooooo! Not again! Not Daddy! Why? Whyyyyyyy??"

I couldn't scream loud enough; I couldn't cry hard enough to come close to the pain I was enduring. I grabbed my chest repeatedly as if trying to reach for the pain inside me to throw it as far away as possible.

I knew God heard me. Even in my darkness, even when He didn't give me an immediate answer, I knew He heard me. I knew all of Heaven heard me. But were they crying with my sisters and me? Then I felt a physical touch. I was being held. My hair was being stroked. I heard sobbing in my ear as I was being held, rocked, and soothed.

I don't remember how we got back to Lauderdale that evening. But there we were, standing in the bedroom that the three of us shared. Sandy told us that in the morning, Daddy would be brought to the house and stay in the parlor until the funeral, which was set for the upcoming weekend.

Then Ellen, Lulu, and I fell asleep in our only bed.

PARLOR

Daddy was delivered in the morning. *Delivered. That sounded so weird.*

Sandy encouraged all of us to spend time with him. She, Ellen, and Lulu did so throughout the day. But not me. I stood in the hallway, looking into the parlor at Daddy's open casket, but I didn't go in.

Later that night, I stood in front of the parlor door. I just stood there.

Ellen came up behind me and scolded, "Go in there! You haven't been in there all day!"

"I know! …I will! …OK! Just– just leave me alone!" I hesitated and cried.

"Go, Karlin! What are you afraid of?"

"I'm NOT afraid!" I hissed.

Ellen turned the doorknob, opened the parlor door, and shoved me in. "Then get in there."

I tripped on the rug and stumbled in. When I righted myself, I still stood away from Daddy's casket and stared.

Ellen came in too and went straight to Daddy's side. "Get over here," she motioned to me.

HUNG UP

Two weeks earlier, Dad called me at school. He asked how I was doing and about my grades, and we talked about my worst subject, Algebra. – You know, the stuff that's more important to parents. But then we argued. And I don't remember what it was about. It could have been something about clothes or shopping, and Daddy telling me to save up my weekly allowance for it.

I got mad. I was being a sappy, bratty teenager, and I hung up on him.

JUST ME

The last time I talked to my dad, I hung up on him. And now I was facing him in his casket. The guilt I was riddled with weighed a thousand pounds.

The parlor was dimly lit only by the light from oil lamps, as Dad and Sandy had designed. The room was elegantly furnished with antique pieces and turn-of-the-century décor. Flowers from the community began to arrive. The parlor started to resemble a Victorian funeral home—somewhat eerie, but undeniably beautiful in a vintage way. Dad was resting amidst his work, the dream he'd been building with Sandy.

Lulu appeared in the parlor, and now Jim's three girls were by his side. We all leaned in to examine our dad, to check for any visible injuries, and to memorize him forever. – He was wearing his Levi Garrett chewing tobacco baseball cap and had a bag of chew tucked into his left shirt pocket. That was Jim Davis's daily look. And it was very fitting. However, his hands were both wrapped up. We were told that Daddy's hands were badly injured.

We talked among ourselves and even with Daddy. Then Ellen and Lulu left, leaving just me. I closed the door and moved back to Daddy's side.

At first, I just looked at him quietly until the tears welled up. Then I broke down crying.

"Daddy … I'm so sorry I hung up on you." I cried. "I'm so sorry I didn't tell you 'I love you' on the phone. I'm sorry I haven't made things easy for you and …"

The hard candy I'd been sucking on rolled out of my mouth, followed by a string of spit, and fell into the casket as I was ugly crying.

I blinked hard to clear my eyes and hurried to find it before anyone walked back in. I leaned in deep and looked all around as closely as possible.

"Daddy, hold on … I—I lost my candy …"

Now I was feeling all around inside the casket.

"Found it!" It landed in a fold on Daddy's shirt sleeve. *Whew!*

I held the green apple Jolly Rancher up to the lamp light, plucked a few fuzzies off of it, looked down at Daddy with a goofy grin, and put it back in my mouth.

I stood by Daddy a little longer. My playful grin faded back to a somber look. I looked at his peaceful face, remembering how hard he struggled with Sandy's and my bitter relationship, and when he once cried, telling me that he didn't know what else to do to bring peace between us.

"That's why I went to French Camp, Daddy," I whispered. "I hope things got better for Sandy and you after I left."

I started crying again, but a peace came over me.

"I love you, Daddy. I always have. I don't know what to do without you. A girl needs her Daddy, you know? But I'll figure it out."

A tear rolled down my nose and dropped on my Daddy's shirt near his heart. With that, I kissed him on his forehead, his cheek, and his nose.

"I will miss you forever."

Over the next few days, Jim's daughters spent more quiet moments alone with him before the funeral. But this time was my 'goodbye'—my moment to come to terms with being an orphan and how to navigate life from here on out.

ANOTHER ONE

Funeral day had arrived. Daddy's casket was brought outside to the front yard and placed under a canopy in front of several rows of chairs, atop a large indoor/outdoor faux-grass rug.

We wouldn't be the Davises if we didn't have animals. Thanks to Sandy and Lulu, we were stray cat central. Six or seven cats wandered around the chairs, the casket, and between people's feet until the chickens showed up.

Front and center, they strutted in from the backyard, curious about what in the tarnation was going on. They surely ruled the roost, in more ways than one, and the cats knew it. The felines made way for them, keeping a safe distance up in a tree or retreating to the front porch, perched on the banister or lounging on the swing and rockers. Lulu said those chickens were straight-up buttholes.

After the eulogy, Sandy draped herself on Daddy's casket, embracing it. She whimpered, whispered to her husband, and cried. I watched intently through my tears as a wife grieved her husband. My heart ached for her. No matter our differences, even when she was my enemy many times, I hated all of this for her.

Daddy's parents were there, Grandma Jessie and Grandpa Charlie Davis. His two sisters came as well, but his little brother couldn't bear it.

Men were coughing, women were sobbing, sniffling, and blowing their noses. It's a sad day when a neighbor helps a stranger only to be crushed by a drunk driver. – My dad survived Vietnam and bullets whistling past his ear many times. But kindness, somehow, killed him. Life just doesn't make sense like that.

The Honor Guard gave a command.

I put on some lip gloss while turning around in my chair to see who attended and—

POW!

Holy Mary, mother of God! The devil went down to Georgia!! I jumped out of my skin! – Cats yowled, hissed, and scattered in all directions, their claws getting stuck in the rug as they dug in for traction. Chickens squawked, jumped, flapped their wings, ran in circles, and disappeared. – It was chaos in the animal kingdom!

In the aftermath, tufts of cat fur and feathers hung in swirling suspension in the air before floating daintily to the ground.

A rooster crowed.

POW!

I covered my face, giggling so hard, trying to keep quiet. A little feather landed on my mouth and stuck to my lip gloss. And I accidentally blew a snot bubble.

POW!

I knew about the 21 Gun Salute. But I thought I had a few more seconds.

Taps played. They folded the American flag and gave it to Sandy.

CHAPTER 12
Life Goes On

POOF Ellen and I were back at French Camp again.

I wanted to stay home longer, but the Dean convinced us to return for our final exams. Ellen wasn't a big fan of Mr. Newman, but she somehow felt safe with him and was eager to go. I think the school was worried that we might not want to come back the longer we stayed away. That's understandable. But I had a cute boyfriend. OF COURSE, I'd return. I just wanted to stay home a little longer with Sandy. I felt sorry for her.

I remember walking into my dorm room, laying down my luggage, and my best friend Vicki standing nearby in silence, waiting to support me when I needed it. She didn't know what to say, so she didn't say anything, which said so much. I lay on my stomach facing the foot of my bed while Vicki sat on the floor with her back against it, and we talked. She cried with me. And she laughed through tears when I told her about my Jolly Rancher falling into Daddy's casket.

I had a tough time falling asleep for the next three weeks. I stared at the ceiling for hours, thinking and praying.

Mom was only 34, Daddy was just 41. I asked God to let me live to at least 25— Wait. No. Until I got married— No wait. Until I had children, but after I saw my grandchildren grow up. So basically, I asked God if I could live a long and full life, unlike my parents.

One night, I didn't sleep at all. The next night, I grew frustrated because I wasn't feeling sleepy and couldn't understand why my heart was racing. Then, on the following night, I started trembling as if I were cold, even though I wasn't.

I knocked on my dorm parent's door, wrapped in a blanket.

"I can't sleep. And I can't stop shaking," I said.

Mrs. Ainsworth made me some hot chocolate and talked with me until I felt sleepy.

Little did I know that my mind and body were trying to cope with trauma, which gave way to anxiety.

NOT THE SAME

That first night back at FCA blurred into Thanksgiving—the first one without Daddy.

I don't remember exactly how it went, but I do remember my sweet boyfriend telling me, as I was getting ready to go home, "Remember, Karlin. This is your first Thanksgiving without your dad. It's not going to be the same."

Oh! And I also remember Lulu coming back to French Camp with us.

We were all together now.

"So, what dorm is she going to?" I asked my dorm mother while Sandy and Lulu were going through the admissions process.

"She's coming to Griffin," Mrs. Ainsworth replied with a laser-focused stare.

And she added, "Since you girls just lost your dad, we thought it would be best if we put her in here with you." *You did WHAT?!?*

"Um... Why???

"Because you're her sister, Karlin."

"So?... Put her with Ellen in Heidelberg. Why me?"

"Because you're the eldest." *Not the first-born reason for everything.*

"Uh, we don't get along, you know! We're gonna fight!" I warned.

"Be the example, Karlin. Make it work," Mrs. Ainsworth said as she closed my bedroom door behind her.

It was the worst best intention ever. All my dorm mates thought little Lulu was the sweetest, cutest thing. But I didn't know who that person was! We fought like feral cats every day.

EVERY. DAY.

It wasn't my sinister plan, but after a couple of months, the adults in charge realized it was a bad idea after all, and Lulu was moved to the Spencer-McCain dorm, a home for students her age. *Yessss!*

Mrs. Ainsworth came to my room while I was packing for Spring break.

"Karlin, since you're almost 16, the Judge is letting you decide who you want to have guardianship over you and your sisters: Sandy or French Camp?" she asked.

We stared at each other. Then I inhaled to answer—

"This is a critical decision to make, Karlin," she interrupted, slowly and deliberately. "What you choose now could impact you and your sisters."

Mrs. Ainsworth was an extremely intelligent woman. She knew what I was thinking. French Camp Academy was truly my refuge, but it was very restrictive. I wanted more freedom when I was off campus. And of course, I made my decision based on a boy.

"I choose Sandy…" I said, almost cringing.

Mrs. Ainsworth looked hard at me. Then she clapped her hips with her hands and said, "Ok! … Ok. I'll let the attorney know."

I knew she wasn't pleased with my answer. But I also genuinely felt sorry for Sandy and didn't want to cut ourselves out of her life as quickly as she lost Dad. I thought we could serve as each other's link to him. At least, that's how I saw her. I convinced myself I could make it work for everyone… while having my cake and eating it too.

I told Sandy I chose her.

"You did?" She asked, slightly confused, and seemingly with a hint of disappointment. She looked down, then shook her head. "Well, OK."

I was hoping for a mushier, sappier response than that. But… OK.

BONDING

The four of us bonded, I believe.

Sandy looked after us, cooking while we helped her continue with her and Dad's restoration project. We even all slept together in the same room, talking quietly in the dark.

Sandy was young at heart, and we were catching up to her. I sensed a budding relationship, and I enjoyed it very much. But I also often felt sad and regretful that Daddy was missing out on it. I just don't understand the way God does things.

Spring Break was pleasant.

SPITFIRE

I turned 16, passed all my finals, white-glove cleaned my room, and we went home for the summer.

All packed with a suitcase each, Sandy picked us up…
in a red 1981 Triumph Spitfire.

Read that again.

On the outside, we were all Oooohs and Aaaahs, but on the inside, I was wondering how the three of us and our suitcases would fit in this two-seater convertible. *What the heck, Sandy?!?*

But where there's a will, there's a way, right? We stuffed two suitcases into the tiny trunk, two sisters shared the passenger seat, and one sister sat in the space behind both seats with another suitcase. We drove two hours like that, hoping not to get pulled over.

Sandy seemed carefree with her mane blowing in the wind.

MOVING ON

Summer was interesting.

Sandy had become a social butterfly, going to the NCO club on base and dancing. She dated a guy named Jim for a while. Can we say awkward? I don't know — maybe I was too judgmental at 16 — but dating a guy with the same name as your late husband seemed a bit weird to me.

As Sandy got busy "living", so did my sisters and I.

We went to the First Baptist Church of Lauderdale and picked up where we left off with friends in the youth group.

All summer long, we hung out, played night volleyball at Lake Dalewood or on the church grounds, went on youth group trips, saw movies, and swam in the lake. That was our nightlife. No drugs. – Well, maybe one joint and an occasional cigarette just to look cool. I swear, I didn't inhale! It was just a prop. I didn't want to cough up a lung from inexperience, and I really was a scaredy cat. – And no alcohol. – Well, maybe one small glass of Southern Comfort and Mountain Dew that I didn't finish as we wandered through a house party, of which the parents weren't home. Rich kids. Must be nice.

That was the summer of "An Officer and a Gentleman."

Sandy took us to see it, even though she had already watched it seven times. Daddy wasn't a Naval Aviator, but he still looked handsome in his dress whites and summer blues. I think Sandy just wanted to relive the nostalgia of being a Petty Officer's wife.

It was also the summer of Sasha, a baby boa constrictor that Sandy brought home one day.

My sisters and I weren't squeamish about having a pet snake. We actually enjoyed the fact that the community knew, thought we were weird, called Sandy the Crazy Snake Lady, and avoided us on the street.

Instead of a "Beware of Dog" sign, Sandy put up one that said "Beware of Snake" in the front door window.

Then, to really drive her point home – I'm weird. STAY AWAY! – Sandy took Sasha to the gas station/convenience store/laundromat, allowing her to slither around her arms and shoulders while showing employees and customers.

Believe me, that display and the sign on our door were more effective than any deadbolt lock.

I still arranged my transportation with the church and went on my own.

One Wednesday evening, as I was taking the church van home, I was talking with Mrs. Wiggins, the driver and assistant youth group leader. We were talking about how God works differently in everyone's lives, and how He is always faithful to provide.

I agreed, sharing how God has always provided for my sisters and me, making a way for us when there was no visible path.

"For example," I said. "When our Mom died, God immediately sent us to our Dad. Then God established us at the boarding school. So when our dad died, we were already there, and my baby sister joined us a week later. Now we're all together again, being raised in the Lord at the school. At the time, I couldn't see it. But I can definitely see His hand in everything now. God always had someone or something in place for us when a huge change was coming in our lives. He's been taking care of us all along—a father to the fatherless—especially in all our troubles and struggles."

I caught Mrs. Wiggins looking at me curiously through the rear-view mirror. She didn't say much. Just kept nodding her head and driving. I don't know if I was rambling or if she wasn't expecting what I said.

I kind of wasn't expecting what I said either.

CHANGING

As summer went on, Sandy started to change. Her attitude became more negative; she began bashing all men just for having XY chromosomes.

One night, while we were all sleeping in the same room and having our usual nightly conversations, Sandy said something like "Yeah, all men are like that. Just like your dad—" and I don't remember her exact words, only that they were negative. I didn't care. Daddy was her husband, and Sandy knew him differently from the way my sisters and I did. So, whatever she said didn't bother me at all.

But then I piggybacked on her thought.

"One summer, when we were all swimming in the pool, I came into the house to get more towels and saw Mom sitting on Daddy's lap. I didn't even know he was visiting! And I thought Mom hated Dad-"

Ellen nudged me under the covers.

Sandy was quiet. I could not believe I had just blurted that out. I didn't mean to. I didn't even want to. It just rolled off my tongue with no thought whatsoever. And now I can't take it back, I can't rewind time. I'm such an idiot! WHAT WAS I THINKING?!?
You weren't thinking, Karlin! That's the problem.

Sandy got up quietly. She fumbled in the dark for a vinyl record and played music by The Supremes on her record player, "Play a Sad Song." Her shadow swayed slowly to the music as the moon shone through the window. Then she sniffled and went into the next room.

Ellen punched me under the sheets. *I deserved it.*

"Why did you say that?!?" she hissed.

"I don't know! I don't know! I didn't mean to!" I insisted. "I wasn't thinking—"

"You never think, Karlin!" Ellen growled. "Gahh, you're so stupid!"

About 15 minutes later, Sandy came back into the room and crawled under her covers.

"I'm sorry, Sandy," I whispered. "I don't know where that came from. I just remembered it and blurted it out accidentally. I did not mean to hurt you."

"It's Ok … I told you, all men are like that."

More and more, Sandy was staying out all night long, coming home before sunrise, and sleeping all day.

She shopped for groceries less and less, and the fridge and cupboards were getting bare. Sandy would come home in the mornings and toss each of us a gas station/convenience store/laundromat BBQ sandwich. And we were very excited to get that.

Sandy slept all day and woke up grumpy until she got ready to go out again, dressed up with glitter and sequins. She was starting to act like an out-of-control teenager … except the real teenagers in the house weren't acting like that.

I didn't know what kind of nightlife Sandy was living, but she became careless, leaving her purse open in the bathroom, exposing wads of money.

One morning, Sandy was already fast asleep when I took my morning bath. I stared at all that money she had in her purse. I didn't count it, but I was certain she wouldn't notice a $10 bill missing. So, I took it. And bought food for my sisters. When I spent it all, I took a $20 bill the next time. Was I stealing? … *maybe*.

My sisters and I took turns walking to the Post Office to check the mail every day. Ellen and I were aware of the government checks for each of us every month: James L Davis FOR Karlin K Davis, Sandra A Davis FOR Karlin K Davis, etc. These were Social Security Survivor benefits. Two checks came for each of us every month. Money that was meant to take care of us.

Since Sandy stopped buying groceries, I kept taking what my sisters and I needed from her purse. Therefore, no, I was not stealing. … *technically*.

STAY OUT

One night, as Sandy was getting ready to go out, she stormed out of the bathroom and demanded, "ARE YOU GUYS TAKING MONEY OUT OF MY PURSE?!?"

"Yes," I said.

"STAY OUT OF MY F------G PURSE, KARLIN!"

"Then buy groceries, Sandy." I flatly said. "There's no food in the house."

"I'm not going to say it again! STAY OUT OF MY PURSE!"

"BUY GROCERIES AND I WILL!" I countered.

Sandy threw a $20 bill at me and stormed out of the house.

Whatever relationship I thought was budding had just withered.

One night, Sandy dressed up like a drag queen. I'm not sure if that was her intended look, but none of us was going to tell her otherwise. The next night, she dressed country and wore a cowboy hat. It turned out she was working as a DJ at a local bar, which explained her nightlife and her daytime sleeping schedule. I think. Judging by the rolls and wads of money in her purse, she must have played some outstanding music.

FIRST DRUNK

One night out, I split off from my churchy friends and did something out of character with another person. She had a bottle of wine and offered me some.

Wine. Hmm. I didn't think that was what most teens were drinking, but I guess we were classy and refined teens. It was really sweet. Wow! Like, grape juice sweet. I liked it! I drank the whole bottle! It was something duck. Swan? Duck, swan, something? I don't remember. Anyway, when my friend took me home, for some reason I kept tripping and falling, so she walked me up the steps to the front porch.

Ellen opened the door, unimpressed as usual. I giggled, and Ellen rolled her eyes with disgust and dragged me inside.

"YOU REEK! ARE YOU DRUNK?!?" She yelled.

"No! … I dunno? … SHHHHHHHHHHHHHH! Is Sandy home?" I spat and slurred.

"Of course not. And you're lucky!" she said as she dragged me into the bedroom and shoved me onto the bed.

"You're so stupid. SLEEP IT OFF!" She said and returned to watching MTV.

In perfect harmony, at the worst possible time, everything happened all at once.

I sat up in bed, holding my tummy, moaning.
"… Ohhhhh, I don't feel good. I think I'm gonna--"

Headlights flashed down the hallway through the front door window, and a car slowly drove over gravel.

"Shit! Sandy's home!" Ellen grabbed me and dragged me to the bathroom, but not before I bumped into the huge marble pedestal table in the middle of the hall, doubled over it, and barfed. I didn't even heave. I just opened my mouth and out rolled sour grape lava.

"KARLIN?!?" Ellen panicked. She peeled me off the table and dumped me on the bathroom floor.

"Don't come out!" she commanded.

Then she grabbed a towel and threw it over my vomitus, wiped it up, and threw the towel away.

"Oh God <gag> I'm sorry, <panting> I'm so sor— <heave> I promise, I'll <gag, puke> I'll never do this again, just <heave> get me through this. <panting> Please Lord <puke, heave, heave>" I prayed over and over while I white-knuckled the cold porcelain throne so I wouldn't fall off the planet as it spun on its axis.

The front door opened and closed. Ellen was talking to Sandy.

"Ew. What's that smell?" Sandy asked.

"Karlin's sick," Ellen covered. "I think she didn't cook the chicken all the way." *Genius!*

"Yep! That'll do it." Sandy knocked on the bathroom door and said, "I told you, 'You gotta cook meat well, especially chicken'."

"I know, I kno— <gag, heave, hurrrrrl – fart – hurrrrrrl, snort>."

Sandy went to bed. We didn't see her again until sunset, like a vampire.

It was a beautiful sunny day when I finally emerged from the bathroom and staggered back to bed.

My first drunk. *YUCK!*

BRAWL

A few weeks before summer ended, when Sandy went out for the night, Ellen and I did too. We hung out at the lake and played volleyball with friends until well past midnight.

Lulu stayed home. She didn't have much fun with our friends and was happy to stay home with the animals and read.

We arrived home at our usual time, around 2 a.m. But oddly enough, Sandy beat us this time. She met us in the hallway, and a big fight broke out. Sandy was furious that we went out and left Lulu at home. She was screaming at us, and we screamed back.

"You and Daddy left Lulu home alone every time y'all went out to dinner! What's the difference?" Ellen yelled.

"We were never gone very long!" Sandy yelled back. "You two left her *all* night!"

Lulu stepped into the doorway of our bedroom. "Y'all, really, it's okay. I didn't—"

"She was younger! And she was scared!" I yelled at Sandy. "Don't act as if you care now!"

Sandy turned around and charged me. "I've had it with you, you little whore!"

She hit my jaw with a closed fist, and I fell against the wall.

Ellen kicked Sandy in her hip from behind. "Leave her alone!"

Sandy spun around and punched Ellen in the eye.

Lulu screamed. "STOP! STOP FIGHTING!"

Sandy spun around again, raised her fist, and charged Lulu.

Ellen screamed, "DON'T YOU TOUCH HER!"

I grabbed Sandy's long hair, wrapped my hands around in it, and pulled it as hard as I could.

Then Ellen hit Sandy in the chest.

And somehow, all three of us fell back away from each other as if something exploded or pushed us apart.

We were all panting. Lulu was sobbing.

"Pack your shit," Sandy said. "You're all going back to French Camp."

Sandy dropped us off at the Greyhound bus station just before dawn. The summer before my junior year was cut short.

Back in our respective dorms, Mr. Ainsworth looked at my jaw.

"Yeah, she clocked 'ya real good," he said. Then he asked me to move my jaw one way, then the other, and then to clench.

Mrs. Ainsworth watched, barely shaking her head enough for me to understand she disapproved of all this. She was right.

"Barely," I said, as my jaw returned to its crooked place.

It took about a week for my jaw to go back to normal, and I could finally chew meat.

Ellen's black eye healed in about the same time.

CHAPTER 13
Junior

The fall of my junior year was in full swing.

Sandy came to the school on a Friday night and watched me cheer at a home football game. The last time she attended a game was with Daddy when I was a freshman. I'm not sure if she was trying to keep that going, like a tradition of some kind. If so, it was a thoughtful gesture. But it was very awkward! For one, we never talked about the fight we had in the summer. I needed some kind of resolution, some closure. Without it, things just felt weird.

Our relationship with Sandy had morphed into a symbiotic one. Hers was the go-to house when we weren't at French Camp, and she depended on our benefits checks. Yep. Things had definitely changed.

SASHA

When we went home for Thanksgiving, I placed my suitcase in our bedroom. Something hanging between the top of the curtain rod and the wardrobe caught my eye.

Oh, that's new, I thought. I wondered what kind of Victorian decor that was. I turned my head sideways and pondered. I squinted. Then I slowly turned my head to look at the 120-gallon snake habitat on the floor in the corner of our room.

"Sandy? … Where's Sasha?" I hollered.

"I dunno. She got out." Sandy hollered back from another room.

I'm not squeamish about snakes, but that thing hanging from the window to the wardrobe was Sasha's shed skin, which means she got bigger. Not knowing where a boa constrictor is in your bedroom is concerning, especially since it was cold, so she'll be looking for a warm place to sleep. Sandy often let Sasha sleep with her, but I sure wasn't sleeping with any snake!

"Nope, I'm not sleeping in this room," I said and walked out with my suitcase. I don't remember where I slept in the house that night, but it wasn't in that room.

HEATER

It was a chilly November; the house was cold. We weren't allowed to turn on the gas heater in our bedroom.

But when our fingers and toes started to hurt, Ellen asked Sandy if we could turn on the heater.

"No! Gas costs money!" she barked as her room was warm and cozy from her gas heater.

Ellen stood firm. "Why? Your heater is on while we're freezing. And you have the TV. How come we have nothing?"

Sandy rolled her eyes. "Fine!" And she turned our heater on.

Deja vu? Seven years ago, Sandy ate cookies in front of her fiancé's 8-year-old daughter and refused to share. As time goes on, it's a universal expectation that everyone will grow up, learn, and change. Sandy hadn't. But Ellen didn't take no for an answer this time.

Christmas came and went. Other than Victorian decorations, nothing else was new with Sandy. Our lives seemed to settle into this pattern.

SPRINGBREAK 1983

Ellen went to her roommate's house for spring break, so it was just me and Lulu at home.

The very next day, Sandy headed for Virginia to visit a friend. – There was no food in the house, and Lulu came to me, scared and crying, "We're going to starve, Karlin! We have nothing!"

She was right. Not only did we have no food, but I had no money. I had to figure something out.

"No, we're not, Lulu," I reassured her. "I'll be right back. Stay put."

"Where– where are you going?" Lulu asked as she wiped her tears.

"I'm going to Miller's store."

Miller's General Store & Mercantile was a tiny, small-town mom-and-pop store just down the road and over the railroad tracks, a few rundown shacks away from Sandy's antique shop.

I knew that Miller's wasn't letting Sandy charge anymore because she hadn't paid her last tab. But desperate times called for desperate measures. I was willing to beg, even to the point of ugly crying, complete with snot bubbles. Whatever it took.

As expected, Mrs. Miller told me no. "I'm sorry, darlin', but I can't open a tab for you. Sandy still has one outstanding."

She called me 'darlin', but that wasn't out of sweetness. That's just standard Mississippi talk – she was very flat and unaffected by our plight, which Sandy created. So, I had to turn it up a notch.

"I know, Mrs. Miller," I answered … with a cracking voice. "But Sandy left us with absolutely nothing and no money," I cued the tears.

"And Lulu is crying herself sick." I blinked, and the first tear rolled down my cheek.

"I'm not Sandy, Mrs. Miller. But I promise–" I blinked again, and another tear dropped. "My tab will get paid!" Then I held up my fist to emphasize my promise, and I strengthened my voice like … Scarlet O'Hara.

Mrs. Miller put her hands on her hips and said, "Now, just how are you going to do that, young lady?" – She knew I lived at the boarding school and didn't have a job.

I paused. And remembered the Post Office.

"I check the mail every day, Mrs. Miller," I said.

She looked at me and tilted her head.

"I don't have money now, but I'll have access to money when Sandy gets back. And I promise, both tabs will get paid."

I turned the sadness back on to seal the deal. "Please, Mrs. Miller?"

She closed her eyes, shook her head, and grumbled, "Oh, bless you child … I ain't never heard of a mother–"

"Step" I corrected.

"STEPmother leaving her kids without any food!... That's just fool hearted!" Mrs. Miller continued grumbling while she filled a brown paper bag with some items.

"Here you go, darlin'," now she meant it sweetly. "All I can spare is 2 pounds of bologna and 2 loaves of bread," and she handed the bag to me.

But before letting go of it, she looked at me long, and I stood there and let her. I saw sadness in her eyes for my sisters and me.

"Thank you so much, Mrs. Miller. Thank you with all my heart." I reached out to squeeze her hand. And the next teardrop was genuine.

Lulu and I ate dry bologna sandwiches for ten days. No mayo. No mustard. Just bread and bologna. But we were so thankful.

I checked the mail and hid one of the benefit checks with my name on it. This was my leverage to make Sandy pay our bills when she returned. I watched enough cop shows to know that was illegal, but I was desperate.

I didn't know what I'd do if my plan went sideways. I mean, I was tiny; Sandy could easily pummel me if she wanted to. But it was a risk I had to take.

Sandy came back the night before Lulu and I had to go back to FCA. She thumbed through the mail I left her on the dining table.

"HEY! … I'M MISSING A CHECK!" She yelled from the dining room.

I stepped into the dining room doorway.

"I have it," I said.

"Why??? … YOU CAN'T CASH IT! It's made out to me!"

"I know," I said plainly. "But I have a small tab at Miller's–"

Sandy looked surprised to hear that.

"And you need to pay *both* tabs off, Sandy."

She did not like that I knew about her unpaid tab.

"ALRIGHT KARLIN!" Sandy barked with indignation.

I placed Sandy's check on the dining room table and went back to my room.

SUMMER 1983

It was the summer of the movie "Flashdance." Leg warmers and off-shoulder sweatshirts were trendy, along with lace, giant hair bows, headbands, and Madonna's mismatched fashion. I even had a Joan Jett layered haircut with a little spike on top, defying French Camp's rule against faddish hairstyles.

It was my last summer before my Senior year. We spent our summer at FCA, but we came home for the first 2 weeks after school let out, and the last 2 weeks before the next semester started.

While Sandy was being Sandy, I spent our lazy two weeks sunbathing in the yard:

Lawn chair, check.
Boombox, check.
Hawaiian Tropic dark tanning oil, check.
Reflective tanning blanket, check.
Sun-In or lemon juice, check.
Water sprinkler positioned to rain on us, check.

Even though I already had some melanin, darker was beautiful to me.

It was during these two weeks that Sandy went on another road trip. Again? I noticed a pattern.

"What do you need?" She asked us.

"Open a tab at Miller's store so I can get groceries," I said.

Sandy amicably agreed. She must have squared away our tabs from spring break after all. And for nearly two weeks, I cooked up some chicken-fried steak, shepherd's pie, spaghetti, chili, beef stew, and even some fried rice. We were eatin' good!

Were we afraid of being left alone again? No. I was 17 now, Sasha kept intruders out, and Ellen and I knew how to use Daddy's guns if Sasha didn't hold up her end of the deal. We also had a phone—on the wall, with a rotary dial and a very long curly cord—with plenty of people to call if we needed to.

When Sandy came home, she threw a fit about the tab.

"DAMN KARLIN! WHAT DID YOU BUY?" She yelled.

"Groceries," I said matter-of-factly.

"You probably ate junk while I was gone!"

"No, Sandy, I bought good food. And there's more in the fridge and cabinets for you to cook with if you want to."

"Oh…" She mumbled and left the room.

Sandy never apologized for anything. I never heard her say she's sorry. If she was wrong about something or someone corrected her and she knew it was right, all she would say is "...oh."

EXPECTATION

When we returned to Lauderdale for the final two weeks before the new school year began, my sisters and I were lounging in our one-bed bedroom, chatting.

Sandy came in and inserted herself into our conversation. We didn't mind. We always welcomed her, despite our tainted relationship. We were always hopeful like that.

After a few minutes of meaningless chatter, Sandy stood at the end of our bed to make an announcement.

"Ok, ok, listen!..." She started with a playful demeanor and smile—an uncommon sight.

We hushed and gave her our undivided attention.

"Ok… Since your trust funds will be sizable by the time each of you turns 21, I expect $10,000 from each of you!" She was still smiling.

There was a pause. It was uncomfortable. And Sandy's smile started to twist a little.

I broke the silence. "You want us to give you $30,000 of our Mom's money?" I asked for clarification in the most composed tone.

"Mmhmm," She renewed her smile with a hint of nervousness. "What do you need it for?" I asked with focus. "Why that amount?"

"Uh– I don't know. I just threw a number out there. I could pay off some bills with it, you know?" Sandy grew uneasy and began fidgeting with her hair.

"That's a lot of money, Sandy," I said in a very flat and even tone. "Like, paying the school's tuition?"

Sandy hadn't paid our tuition in a year. So the school found sponsors for the Davis sisters. It was the only way they could keep us sheltered until we were 18. To go home for the holidays and semester breaks was one thing. But for us to leave French Camp completely and be in Sandy's "care" was unconscionable to them. – And Sandy didn't know that I knew.

"I just thought y'all could spare– Like, maybe we could– How did you – Oh NEVERMIND!... I was just asking!" Sandy was completely flustered and couldn't complete her thoughts.

She threw her hands in the air as if she'd had enough of our unfair interrogation practices and mistreatment, and stomped out of our room, embarrassed.

"We'll think about it, Sandy," I said with a tiny sliver of hope, as her hair swooshed my face as she flung it while storming past me.

"I said NEVERMIND!" She yelled from the hallway.

I looked at Ellen and Lulu lying on the bed. Ellen shook her head no. Lulu shrugged her shoulders.

"I'm not giving her jack crap," I muttered.

***

The audacity!... The narcissism!... The gall!...
I could go on, and on, and on! She called that "just asking"?!?
She didn't pay our tuition; she barely fed us; she didn't buy us clothes; but she collected our survivor benefits —and she had bills???

AND SHE *EXPECTED* $30K FROM OUR MOM'S TRUSTFUNDS?!?

ARE YOU KIDDING ME?!?

I should have listened to Mrs. Ainsworth.

CHAPTER 14
Senior

It was my senior year. Time to get serious about the future and adulthood. College? Ok. Maybe. I know that's what Daddy would have wanted.

I remember the summer before he passed, he asked me what I wanted to do when I grew up.

"I want to be a good wife, Daddy," I said.

Daddy took off his glasses and rubbed the bridge of his nose. "Peanut, that's very admirable," he said. "But what if, God forbid, something happens to your husband?"

"Well … hopefully nothing will," I said.

"Hopefully. But, what if" he pressed.

I looked at him blankly, and I think Daddy started to lose a little faith.

"Peanut, if you're ever left without a husband, you're going to need something to fall back on. A college education would be excellent to have for that." *Great. More math.*

When Daddy retired from the Navy, he began taking classes at the local junior college. It turned out I was already studying the same level of algebra in high school.

One day, while he was doing his homework, I stood beside his desk and told him about my struggles with math.

"Daddy, I don't think I'm going to pass Algebra this semester."

"Why not, Peanut?"

"I'm failing tests."

Dad looked over his reading glasses at me. "What are you struggling with?"

"I dunno, Daddy. I turn in all my homework, and I love it when I know what I'm doing. But on the tests, I just bomb them," I explained.

Dad paused and reflected for a moment. What he said then changed my view of education forever.

"Are you learning it, though?" He pushed his math book in front of me. "Can you solve this equation?"

"I think so …" I said, using his pencil. He checked my work and my answer, and it was correct.

"Then that's all I care about, Peanut. As long as you learn it."

My jaw dropped as I processed what Daddy had just said, as the weight of quadratic equations, degrees of polynomials, integers, exponents, radicals, and square roots rolled off my shoulders like Atlas drop-kicking the globe.

Granted, I still needed to pass Algebra (and I did). But the confidence I gained from his understanding and perspective was liberating! I felt freed from the shackles of a letter grade.

Interesting, isn't it, how the truth does the same thing? Sets you free?

Dad smiled, winked at me, and went back to work.

Despite everything, my senior year was as wonderful as it could have been.

I was a cheerleader, one of two Homecoming Maids in our class, part of a drama group and was cast in several plays, an alto in the chorus, made honor roll in the last semester, and had a high school sweetheart whom I married six months after graduation (and who is the father of my four sons).

With nothing else to compare it to, my senior year at a Christian boarding school was epic, and life was as grand.

My sights were set forward.

CHAPTER 15
Commence Adulting

I went back to Lauderdale after graduation. My boyfriend went back to Texas. Within a couple of weeks of being home, I started talking to Sandy about the possibility of going to the local junior college, per Daddy's wishes.

"How are you going to pay for it?" she asked me.

I honestly had no clue. Most of my friends had been having these dynamic conversations with their parents throughout the year. But not me and Sandy. Of course not. That would be too logical and responsible.

"–I don't know," I said.

"Well, you'd better figure it out," she exhaled her cigarette. "I ain't giving you any money."

"Can you at least help me figure it out?" I asked.

She was so belligerent. "Girl, you are 18 years old! FIGURE IT OUT! Not one damn person helped me out when I was your age! NOT ONE! I was on my own at 18!"

About a week later, Sandy asked me what I was going to do about getting a job. I told her that the convenience store/gas station/laundromat wasn't hiring. Neither was the little mom-and-pop corner store nor the small bank branch. And the Post Office said I had no experience. All four were within walking distance of our house.

"Hmm. So, what are you doing? What's your plan?" She asked.

"Well, I'm going to have to go into Meridian if I want a job. However, I don't even have a driver's license. But I did take Drivers Ed, so I do know how to drive!" I said with a cheery hopefulness. "Can you help me with that?"

"Pfft! Help you with what?" Sandy scoffed.

All of my friends received some form of help from their parents, whether big or small, to help them transition into the adult world with responsibilities. This could include allowing them to use their car for commuting to work or school, helping with books, or even contributing to tuition.

I humbly asked, "Could I drive your–"

"HELL NO, YOU CAN'T DRIVE MY CAR! ARE YOU CRAZY?!?" Sandy exploded and laughed maniacally as if I was an idiot for even asking. And maybe I was.

I looked down, closed my eyes, and shook my head as I exhaled. "Sandy, I need a job. But I have no transportation." I tried reasoning with her.

She took a long drag from her cigarette, then stared at me through the exhaled smoke.

"Karlin ... I think it would be best if you found other living arrangements." *Really?*

As I was processing what she had just said, Ellen walked into the parlor where Sandy and I were talking.

"Are you kicking Karlin out???" Ellen asked boldly.

I looked at Sandy. She didn't answer and just kept staring at us while smoking. Ellen and I glanced at each other, and I shrugged my shoulders.

Ellen looked back at Sandy. "Wow ... " she said with utter disgust.

I went into our bedroom and started packing my suitcase. I didn't have much.

"Where are you going to go?" Ellen asked me.

"I'm not really sure. But I'm going to see if I can stay with Gina and her family for now, and start there."

Sandy kicked me out of the house, less than 4 weeks after graduation. And that's how I was catapulted into the world.

With no money and basically homeless, with only a suitcase to my name, I stayed wherever I could and made my way to my boyfriend in Texas. – I still wore a promise ring on my finger, and he did propose to me during the Christmas holidays, so technically, we were engaged. Where else could I have gone?

I caught a ride with friends on a road trip to the Dallas-Fort Worth area, and I stayed with another friend in Grand Prairie until my boyfriend flew me down to Austin.

In November 1984, I married my high school sweetheart… because I was pregnant.

SHIPPED

Had she not gotten caught outside her dorm with a boy at night in 1986, Lulu would have graduated from FCA in 1987.

Her boyfriend at the time thought it was a cool idea to sneak over to her dorm. Loosely propping the locked door open, she met him outside and whisper-argued with him to "get out of here!" After he left and she reached for the door, it slowly closed just beyond her reach, locking her outside. Aaaaaaaaand the rest is history.

However, unfortunately, the result of her actions was that she was expelled. "Shipped" was the term we used for expulsion from the school.

Normally, the school sends students home to their parents. But in Lulu's case, FCA sent her to me. Although Sandy would stay Lulu's legal guardian for another 18 months, the school believed it was not in her best interest to send her back to Sandy.

And we fought worse than when we were roommates in Griffin dorm!

I graduated in 1984, Ellen in 1985, and Lulu was shipped in 1986. There were no more Davis girls at French Camp Academy.

CHAPTER 16
Grown Up

Since 1986, neither Ellen nor Lulu has returned to Lauderdale, and since then, the three of us have grown up.

Warp speed, fast forward:

I married three times, divorced twice, and have four sons, two stepchildren (one of each), and nine grandchildren.

Ellen married twice, divorced once, and has six daughters, two stepdaughters, and ten grandchildren, with another two on the way.

Lulu married and divorced twice and has six children — two sons, four daughters — and six grandchildren, with another on the way.

We were definitely fruitful and multiplied.

I, on the other hand, went back to Lauderdale a handful of times.

People have asked me why I would even bother with Sandy. I have many thoughts on that, but I only have a few answers.

One thing was that Sandy was my last connection to Daddy. Visiting her was almost like visiting my dad. It kept his memory alive as I sat in the parlor of the house he bought decades ago and worked so hard to renovate. Every room of the house and every inch of the property held a memory of him. I'd remember what he looked like, sitting on the front porch…

One stormy night, the lights went out all over tiny Lauderdale. With his pipe and rifle, Daddy sat in a rocker on the front porch. Ellen got out of bed, walked to the screen door, and asked what was wrong.

"Nothing, Monster," he said. "Go back to bed."

And she did, with no questions asked. She slept peacefully, like a baby, through the storm.

I yearned for that nostalgia.

Another thing was that Daddy loved her. I'll never understand how he could have loved a woman who hated his children, but I still wanted to honor him by checking on the woman he loved. I didn't want her to feel like Jim's daughters had completely abandoned her.

And yet, another reason is that I might have been hoping to salvage the past and build a relationship with her that we never had.

Why was I still so hopeful, though? Ellen, Lulu, and all of Daddy's family had washed their hands of her. So why was I still holding on? I must have forgiven Sandy, or else why would I want to stay connected?

Yet, I know many people forgive without staying in touch, letting bygones be bygones while caring from a distance. So why can't I just leave it alone?

THE VISITS

I visited Sandy a total of six times since she kicked me out in 1984. However, the visits in 1999, 2011, and 2014 stand out as the most memorable. But not necessarily in a good way. Each time, I had to come up with some excuse for why Ellen and Lulu couldn't (or wouldn't) visit when she asked about them.

Yep, six times in 39 years. Crazy, right? For someone who really wanted to honor her dad and build a relationship with his widow, I was pretty lazy about it. My efforts were pathetic.

1999

By 1999, Sandy had made significant progress on the house project she and Daddy had started.

Of course, at 49, she was in her prime. She did all the carpentry work herself because she was quite a recluse, never asking for help and turning down offers of assistance.

The house was painted a vibrant navy blue with white trim along the edges and banister, and it had a tin roof. As the trees aged, they grew wildly, with low-hanging branches over a very well-manicured lawn dotted with lilies of various kinds. The white picket fence in the front, with its small gate, led to a walkway beneath an arched trellis of honeysuckle, nestled under the canopy of old, towering trees. It was so Southern and charming. The only thing missing was Spanish moss.

Walking up the stairs to the front porch brought you to the front door, where one side of the porch invited you to sit in a white wicker rocker while sipping iced tea on a miserably humid day. The other side beckoned you to sit on the white porch swing and watch a storm roll in — rain torrentially, then clear out.

The front door opened into a wide hallway. It was huge. One year, we had a giant Christmas tree in the middle of that hall. The vintage wallpaper, oil lamps, and heavy velvet curtains hanging from the tall ceilings divided the hallway into front and back sections. These led to two bedrooms on the left, and the parlor, formal dining room, and country kitchen on the right.

During my visit, Sandy had already gutted the bathroom and replaced it with an outdoor privy and a separate bathhouse.

Privy, if you don't know, is just a fancy word for outhouse. The bathhouse required candlelight and several pails of water from the backyard spigot, warmed on the wood-burning stove in the country kitchen. That's a lot of work just to get clean! I don't know what the women with long hair did before 1900, but I had to wash mine separately with the garden hose.

The guest room where I slept was Sandy's old bedroom, complete with a giant antique Victorian four-poster bed and real goose down bedding. She turned off the electricity to the house, so there was no air conditioning. It was sweltering in August, but an evening breeze blew through the open windows, rustling the white eyelet curtains and creating the illusion of coolness. However, it was really the breeze hitting my sweat that made it tolerable enough for me to fall asleep.

"Karlin," Sandy sang my name. "Wake up! I made breakfast."
She pulled the eyelet curtains all the way open to let the sun's rays flood into the room. I barely caught a glimpse of her as she waltzed away.

It was actually nice waking up just after sunrise to the smell of eggs, bacon, coffee, homemade bread, and wood smoke drifting through the air.

I had hoped to sleep in, but I quickly realized that Sandy was doing what she had always wanted to do: fully live in the era. But she had no one to share it with.

I was in her dollhouse, and she was playing with me.

In 2011, Sandy was 61. Her hair was starting to turn gray, she had put on some weight around her hips, and she was missing several front teeth. She made fun of me about being married for the third time, and she still wasn't wearing a bra.

The yard looked a bit neglected, but it gave the house a mysterious, Halloween-like vibe. She had more dogs than I remembered in 2004, and the cats lounging on the porch and on top of her yellow 1972 VW Bug were feral. But she still fed them anyway.

Inside, I caught intermittent whiffs of animal urine. I also noticed the windowsills were covered in dust, cobwebs, and countless dead bugs. It was like she hadn't dusted since 2004.

As we sat in the parlor, she told me how Hurricane Ivan had blown the old magnolia tree out front onto the parlor roof, and how she had fixed everything herself. She was not impressed with the youth her church sent to help with the repairs, calling them lazy and unreliable.

She brought up my being married for the third time by saying, "... I don't know, Karlin. I kind of thought marriage was for life. Isn't it supposed to be forever?"

I inhaled and tried not to roll my eyes, nodding my head in painful, uncomfortable agreement.

"Yes, Sandy. That's definitely how God designed marriage to be."

Then we started talking about Daddy.

Her tone shifted. The memories she recalled were bitter and filled with resentment. I knew Daddy wasn't perfect, but there are things a daughter—regardless of her age—shouldn't know about her dad. Still, I wasn't rude; I just listened, feeling renewed resentment.

Then Sandy brought up my mom. She thought my dad was trying to make my mom jealous by taking her to a bar they used to go to, hoping my mom would see them together. *What? Why? Why are you telling me this?*

Then she told me that my mom was a prostitute in the Philippines, and that's how my parents met. *Ok, I've heard enough!*

Those were unsettling words, and the conversation became very awkward. Sandy never had anything neutral to say about my mom, so I wasn't surprised. I wish I could blame it on old age and senility, but the truth is she was as sharp as ever, and her words were even sharper.

It's almost as if she no longer liked my dad, as if her memories were mostly negative. – Could it be that what I blurted out about my mom and dad years ago contributed to this? Maybe she was deliberately making my visits unpleasant to discourage me from returning. Or perhaps… when I'm on my own, I dig my own rabbit holes and get lost in them.

"Karlin, I want to give you something," Sandy said as she walked to a closet door and pulled something down from the top shelf.

She handed me Daddy's flag, the one that draped over his casket at his funeral. It had never been unfolded, and all the stars lined up perfectly. Sandy had it wrapped in tissue paper and stored in a cloth bag. My eyes widened as I recalled that day.

"Oh wow, Sandy," I said, deeply moved. "Thank you very much."

"You're welcome."

"But why? Why now?"

She shook her head and raised her eyebrows. "I don't know… I just think maybe your dad might like for you to have it now..."

I nodded my head in acceptance. "Well, thank you, Sandy," I emphasized.

Then she continued, "Besides, I don't have anywhere to put it."
Um… ok?

Sandy walked over to her record player, the only thing that didn't belong in that Victorian room, and put on The Supremes—her go-to music. She closed her eyes and started dancing in place to "Come See About Me." Then she began singing along. I quietly watched from the settee, studying her half-smile that emerged from memories of over three decades ago. She was lost in yet another era, so I took that as my cue to leave.

I walked over to her, I quietly said her name and touched her hand. "Sandy?"

With her eyes still closed and dancing, she took my hand, then picked up my other hand and danced a few beats with me. We swung our hands back and forth in rhythm to the chorus, and I giggled.

"I have to go now, Sandy," I said.

She leaned in for a hug and said, "Ok, bye. Thanks for the visit."

We embraced.

"Tell your sisters I said 'hi' and come visit me!"

"I will," I patted her back. "I love you."

"I love you too, Karlin."

Sandy returned to her memories, singing and dancing alone. I picked up the bag with Daddy's flag and stood in the doorway of the parlor to watch Sandy once more. Why couldn't it have always been like this? I closed the front door behind me and walked away.

Shane admired Daddy's flag. He had a special display case made just for his folded flag. Now both of our fathers' flags are proudly displayed side by side in our home.

*** *** ***

Some not-so-fun facts about my and Shane's fathers: their names are Jim. Both served in the military. My dad's birthday is August 12, 1940, while Shane's dad died on August 12, 1997.

2014

In 2014, we were living in Missouri during my 30th high school reunion. Since it was only an eight-hour drive, we decided to go.

While in Mississippi, I visited Sandy with Shane this time. I prepared him to meet her.

"Ok, Honey … Sandy is an eccentric recluse, and she's socially awkward," I began. "She likes to bring up the past as if I were the worst teenager ever; she has a different memory for everything that happened. Just roll with it. Laugh it off. And let's both try to change the subject as smoothly as possible."

Shane nodded his head, listening intently.

"There's no electricity or plumbing in the house. If you need to use the toilet, there's an outhouse in the backyard. Just grab a branch when you go so you can brush the bugs off the seat … ok?"

Shane's eyes got big, and he nodded his head slowly.

"She had a few dogs and a bunch of feral cats the last time I was here. So, heads up."

Shane nodded his head some more, taking mental notes.

"She's missing some front teeth, and she doesn't wear a bra, so try not to look disgusted."

Shane's thoughts were audible now as he slowly looked at me with concern, *"What the heck am I walking into?"*

Shane pulled up next to the rickety white picket fence.

"This?" he asked.

"Yep ... this." I stepped out of the car, carefully stepping around mud, dog poop, and wild grass as I assessed the property.

Four dogs appeared out of nowhere, barking, sniffing the air, alerting Sandy to visitors. I walked up the porch steps when the door opened.

"Karlin?" Sandy said as she stood at the top of the steps. She smiled with surprise, "What are you doing here?" *Oh! She had her teeth fixed. Good for her!*

"I'm visiting you!" I smiled and hugged her.

"Sandy … this is my husband, Shane," I introduced. "Shane, this is Sandy."

Shane held her hand.

"Hi … Nice to meet you, Shane," she said. *Did she just blush?*

"It's a pleasure, Ms. Sandy. I've heard a lot about you."

"Uh-huh! … I bet you have!" She laughed. *Oh, here we go! …*

Sandy invited us in. "I wish you had let me know you were coming," she said.

"I know. I'm sorry. I lost your number," I explained. "Besides, I like surprising you," I teased.

The three of us sat in the parlor. Shane was looking around, fascinated by having just entered the post-Civil War era. Sandy caught me up on the latest tiny-town gossip about who lives where and who died when. I smelled wood rot and rodent urine this time. Shane started coughing.

I asked Sandy if I could give Shane a tour of the house and the property, but she flatly said no. I was a little indignant, but mostly embarrassed, and I huffed with an uncomfortable chuckle.

"Babe, it's ok. Not a big deal," Shane said between coughs.

A dog barked, so I turned to look out the window and noticed the dirty windowsill. Sandy hadn't dusted since 2011, either! I recognized the same dead spiders buried under new ones.

"So, Karlin," Sandy asked. "When I'm dead and gone, what are you going to do with all this? Because all of this is yours and your sisters." *Did you update your will?*

"Well, I don't know, Sandy," I pondered. "Maybe finish what you and Daddy star–"

"Burn it down!" she interrupted. "Burn it all down. This old house ain't worth a damn!"

"What about the antiques?"

"Sell them. But tear this place down. All of it. And split it with your sisters."

I looked around the parlor and briefly out the window at the overgrown yard. "Ok … if you say so."

Shane's coughing increased, so he excused himself and went outside.

"He's got allergies and asthma. Something must be triggering it." I told Sandy.

"So Shane's a cop?" She brought up. And I think I noted a hint of disdain.

"Yes," I said. "Well … a federal police chief, actually."

Sandy seemed like she was trying to be impressed, but I knew her heart. She never liked law enforcement after Daddy died.

I could hear Shane still coughing outside and knew he needed his inhaler, which we didn't have.

"Sandy, we need to get going," I said.

"Wait. I have something to give you." She stepped out of the parlor, returned with an ornately decorated box, and handed it to me.

Poor Shane was still coughing.

"Something in there triggered my asthma, Babe!" Shane said as we jumped in the car.

"I know. Probably mold. Let's get out of here and get your inhaler."

"Roger that," he agreed. "What's in the box?"

"My dad."

***

Back in Missouri, we placed Daddy's box on the patio table in the backyard and opened it. I had never seen ashes before, and Shane's typical skepticism of people made him want to verify that the box actually contained ashes.

"Yep … those are bone fragments," I whispered as I picked one up. I examined it closely, recalling what I learned about bones in my college Anatomy & Physiology days.

Shane moved Daddy's ashes around with his finger, and a piece of foam and cloth popped up, producing a tiny plume of dust.

"What is that?" I mused.

Shane moved more ash around, uncovering more foam and cloth. We leaned in closer. I gasped.

"This is a silverware box!" I exclaimed. "These foam loops hold the spoons, forks, and knives in place!"

Just then, a breeze blew through, and we quickly shut the box. Shane and I looked at each other and giggled. We both thought of that scene from the movie, The Big Lebowski.

"Sandy couldn't remove the foamy part before dumping Daddy in it?!? Who does that?!?" I said condescendingly.

"The box is beautiful, though," Shane reasoned. "I can see why she wanted to use it. But yeah, I agree. She could have removed the foamy stuff first."

HOME

I only lived in Mississippi for 10 years, but I grew up there, attended high school there, and made lifelong friends there; my two youngest sons were born in Mississippi. So, naturally, Mississippi felt like home to me, even though I'd spent most of my adult life in California.

But one day, Shane and I were talking about retirement. Since the Uintas, Grand Tetons, and Yellowstone were his stomping grounds, Shane eventually wanted us to retire there. However, I was hoping he'd give the Deep South a chance. He curled his lip at the thought, but did say that if a work opportunity presented itself in the southern states, he'd take it.

"If I can, I'll get you as close as possible," he said.

"If not," I countered, "I'll require a lot of land in those mountains."

"Why?" he asked. "And how much land are we talking about?"

"A lot ... so I can be an animal rescue."

"What KIND of animal rescue?"

"All of them."

BACK TO CALI

2015 took us back to California.

We sat around many campfires with our kids, my sisters, nieces, and nephews, planning our exodus from California (again) to build a commune where our whole family could live.

Well, as God would have it, in 2021, Shane's work took us to Prescott, Arizona.

The Kilburns were the first to leave (again), hoping others would follow. But Ellen got a little annoyed and said, "That's not south enough!".

Well… It's a start! *It's a stepping stone, little sister!*

"I promised you I would, Karlin," Shane said. "Jackson, Mississippi. Will that be close enough to your friends?" *Of course!*

I was low-key elated.

"Sweetheart, you don't have to do this. *WE* don't have to do this." I assured Shane. "I don't have to be in Mississippi. I can live anywhere – except Los Angeles – as long as we're together!"

And I meant it, as I was squealing and jumping up and down like a little schoolgirl on the inside.

I left Mississippi *for good* in 1989. Now I'm going back!

But wait, wait, wait!... Shane in Mississippi? I giggled.

And *that*, ladies and gentlemen, is how I ended up back in the Sip.

CHAPTER 17
Handling Affairs

We got back home to Brandon, MS.

Shane could see my gloomy mood and did his best to comfort me.

"Are you going to be ok, babe?" he asked. "I can see a dark cloud over you right now."

"I'll be ok. I'm just processing everything," I reassured him. "I can't tell if I'm sad or ... indifferent. I'm not even sure what 'this' is."

What am I feeling? Or am I numb? Do I even know what emotional numbness feels like?

Well, first things first. Someone's got to contact the funeral home and handle Sandy's affairs. I suppose that's my responsibility? Who else would it be? There's no one else. Sandy had no other relatives. As long as I can remember, she's been estranged from her entire family — the ones she left behind in Big Springs, TX. I don't know of any other family members she might have had.

Oh goodness, what would have happened if I hadn't shown up when I did?

I arranged to return to Lauderdale the following week to go through the house, assess everything, and find her will.

After doing a bit of research in the community – knocking on a few doors on York Rd, asking nosy questions, and looking like a long-lost relative snooping around (which, I kind of was) – I enlisted the help of two of Sandy's neighbors, Marvis and Earl. Marvis had the key to the house and met me there, while Earl walked over from across the road.

"Yeahhh, I tried to date Sandy once. But she was weird," Earl said.

I coughed a laugh as that caught me by surprise, but also because it vindicated me. It wasn't just my sisters and me! Others saw it too.

"Yeahhh, she was lookin' hot back in the day. But then she let herself go, you know," he added.

I paused to look at him; at his belly, at his messy hair and unshaved stubble, at his wrinkled shirt, and dirty jacket.

"Mm hmm," I acknowledged. "Time has a way of doing that to people, Mr. Earl."

Marvis opened the door and …

Urine and some other smells I couldn't identify slammed me in the face and took my breath away. It looked like the house had been abandoned for a long time. When, in fact, Sandy had been living in it just 10 days earlier. Dirt, garbage, and trash everywhere.

A long table was in the middle of the hallway, surrounded by smaller tables, chairs, antique curio cabinets, and anything that could serve as a tabletop. And it was filled with junk.

At the end of the hall, on the floor, were several open cans of cat food, partially eaten and weeks old, next to three very old kitty litter boxes that hadn't been cleaned in months, with litter spilled on the floor all around them. That was one source of stench identified.

I waded carefully through junk and trash on the floor to reach the formal dining room, which looked like a junk storage room amid wall-to-wall antiques.

Then, to the kitchen, it looked like someone or something had emptied a garbage bag on the floor and played in it.

The walls were covered with hundreds of spider webs, each with a hole in the middle. I nearly screamed at the thought of the spiders that spun them; my skin was crawling with the heebie-jeebies, and I didn't dare go any further. NO, THANK YOU!

I was speechless. It didn't look like this in 2014. In 9 years, Sandy became a hoarder, or worse. The living conditions I was standing in looked like a mental illness. I couldn't help but wonder if the filth of the house was what killed her. She was only 73.

I met Marvis and Earl back in the hallway.

"Marvis?!?" I exclaimed. "How could Sandy live like this?!?"

"What you mean?" she asked.

"Like THIS! … All … this!" I motioned everywhere with my hands.

"I don't know. Girl, I ain't never been in here before."

"But … how did you feed her cats? And … how did you find her?"

"When she asks me to, I feed the cats outside. But that morning, when she didn't come to the door, I knew something was wrong, so I went and got Mr. Earl to go inside with me."

I looked at Earl, and he nodded his head.

"So you both found Sandy dead?"

"Yes, ma'am," Marvis said. Earl nodded his head again.

"... Where did you find her?"

Marvis showed me what I remembered as the guest room. That old four-poster bed was still there. But the islet curtains had been replaced with a modern, darker design. It looked like she finally switched to mini blinds, which were battered like the rest of the house.

"I found Ms. Sandy right here. Sleeping. She had her blanket pulled up to her chin. Her head was turned to the side, and she, like, had just a little smile, you know. Like she was at peace, or something." Marvis described. "And there was like a dim light, not a bright light, shining on her face."

"Interesting," I whispered.

I went back to the table in the hallway and said, "I need to find her important documents", and commenced to opening every door, cabinet, and drawer that existed.

Earl went straight to a metal box on the table and opened it.

"This?" he asked.

Lo and behold, Sandy's keys, a few bills, her driver's license, and her will were in that box. Did she know she was dying? Or …

"How did you know about this box, Earl? You found it with a quickness." I know that sounded accusatory, but I didn't mean it to be, and thank God, Earl didn't take it as such.

He shrugged his shoulders and said, "It just looks like a box that someone would put important stuff in. It's the only metal box on this table, so it kinda stood out."

"That makes sense," I agreed.

"Plus, I'm a Vet!" he concluded with military pride.

I opened Sandy's will, and Ms. Marvis and Mr. Earl looked over my shoulder.

It was a short will, front and back. I saw it dated January 1980. And I skimmed it looking for specific names. Nicole, Jenny … Cy and Linda. I turned it over—no other names. I shook the paper out as if what wasn't there would appear. I turned my head sideways and … Nicole, Jenny, Cy, and Linda. I blinked hard. Marvis and Earl were quiet.

I quickly folded up the will, saying, "I'm going to have to reread this and consult my attorney," which I didn't have.

I took the mail out of Sandy's mailbox and thanked Marvis and Earl for their assistance.

Marvis hugged me. "Girl, Sandy sure did love you girls."
I looked up at the sky and rolled my eyes. Only God saw that.

"She used to talk about y'all all the time," Marvis continued. "She missed you girls so much. She used to say, 'This one is doing this, and this one is doing that.' She sure did love y'all." *It's ok, Marvis. You don't have to say all that.*

I drove to the funeral home and gave them all the information they needed for Sandy's death certificate. They were a bit– No, they were *amazed* that I showed up. They weren't expecting anyone.

"Had no one shown up for Sandy, what would y'all have done?" I asked.

The representative cleared his throat. "Well, uhh Mrs. Kilburn, we would have given Sandra a pauper's burial," he said. "But we're so grateful you're doing this for her … because we *know* that you don't have to."

That's right! I don't have to be doing any of this! – I lectured myself on my drive back to Brandon. I'm just a lowly stepdaughter! I'm not even her heir! I'M NOT EVEN IN HER WILL!

I gripped the steering wheel tightly.

Legally, I don't even exist in Sandy's world! So why, Karlin, WHY are you doing this?!? *I don't know …*

If you dumped all this in the garbage right now, nothing would change! Everything would be like yesterday, tomorrow! You could walk away from all this, and your life won't be affected in any way! Let the county worry about the property! You don't need to shoulder this burden! And YOU, of all people, are not responsible for Sandy in any way. Nothing is expected of you. You can walk away from this, and no one would blame you. …*But it doesn't feel like the right thing to do.*

I called Ellen and Lulu. They booked their flights, and I prepared them for what to expect. Then I went online and ordered hazmat suits, masks, gloves, foot covers, hand sanitizer, and several cans of Lysol.

CHAPTER 18
The House

This was the first time since 1984 that the three of us stood on Mississippi dirt together —at the house. It's been 40 years.

If the house could talk, I bet it would be overcome with emotion and cry at the sight of Ellen and Lulu.

> *"Come in, girls! Come in! ... Oh, I've missed you so much! I've missed your footsteps, your hands on the walls, your chatter and giggles, your whispers, and even your fights – and tears. I've watched you struggle and grow. I know it wasn't easy for you. Then you went away and never came back. It's never been the same without you, girls. And as you can see, I'm not the same either. I'm quite dilapidated now. I know you've come back to take care of some unpleasant business, but I'm still so glad to see you again! So, come in, come in! Let me hear your voices once again."*

Seeing my sisters standing in front of the house again filled me with a lot of nostalgic feelings. I won't lie, it was very sentimental for me.

In 1984, I was 18; Ellen, 17; Lulu, 15. We were just girls, for Heaven's sake! This is where we struggled. But look at us now! It didn't break us!

Ellen took it all in with me, nodding her head and smiling. But Lulu looked at the house with a scowl and mumbled some obscenities.

Ms. Marvis joined us, and Mr. Earl hung out with Shane for a while, making small talk.

We opened the trunk of my car and put on the protective garb. We entered the house and began our search for any important documents, anything from our childhood, and anything we wanted to salvage. Ellen was as grossed out as I'd expected. However, Lulu's feral instincts kicked in, and she bulldozed through there on a mission. She knew secret closets and secret drawers within secret closets. If the house had an attic, she would know, because she would have been playing in it back in the day.

Ellen couldn't take it anymore, so she sat in Shane's truck with the dogs. Lulu and I kept going.

When we reached the room where Sandy had passed away, Shane came in to check things out but stood in the doorway.

"What's in that basket on that chair?" Shane asked, pointing.

We all looked, and Marvis said, "Poop paper."

"POOP paper? As in ..." Shane asked, very confused.

"Mm hmm. Cause, you know, sometimes it's too cold to go out back," Marvis explained.

Shane's eyes bulged with horror as he covered his mouth, gagged, and hurried back outside.

I was horrified, too, but thanks to the mask, you couldn't tell.

Lulu was unfazed. I saw it in her eyes—disgusted but unbothered. She's a boss like that.

We found everything we wanted and needed, for now. The three of us stood in front of the house for a moment and just looked at it.

Lulu did the most digging and said, "Did anyone notice that there is no evidence of Dad in the house anymore? None."

I looked at her and agreed. "I noticed."

"Are you ready?" Ellen asked Lulu.

"I think so." Lulu bent down and picked up a couple of rocks and pieces of wood, and Ellen moved out of the way.

In silent contemplation, Lulu threw a rock at the house. Then she threw another rock. She threw a piece of wood, and the glass on the front door shattered.

Lulu stood quietly for a moment. Then she flipped off the house with both hands in a very defiant stance. She started walking away but stopped suddenly to flip it off again, rolling her hands and kicking the air.

"I'm done now," Lulu said. She had her Jenny (Gump) moment. She was satisfied with that closure.

"We good, sister?" Shane asked Lulu.

"I'm good now, little brother."

"Alright then. Let's get outta here."

Sometimes, there *are* enough rocks.

And fingers.

And air kicks.

COMMUNITY

After Ellen and Lulu returned to California, I received a phone call.

"Hi, Marvis! How are you?" I answered.

"Oh, I'm good! I'm good!" she replied. "But listen, I have to tell you something, okay?"

"Sure, what is it?" I asked.

"Girl, I've been hearing things from people, you know. And… Sandy was not nice to you girls. Not nice at all."

I closed my eyes and stiff-lipped a smile.

"No ma'am, she was not, Marvis," I confirmed. "That's why Ellen and Lulu never came back."

"Oh, child, I'm so sorry. I didn't know."

We may have been gone for 40 years, but the community didn't forget the Davis girls.

HOLE IN THE GROUND

Shane and I drove to Lauderdale when Sandy's ashes were ready. We pulled up in front of the house to check her mailbox.

"So what are you going to do with Sandy's ashes?" Shane asked. "Did you want to bury her with your dad when we bury him at the VA cemetery? Or do you want to sprinkle her somewhere?"

"I don't know yet," I said, deep in thought. "I haven't…"

My thought trailed off as I looked out the car window. In clear view was the outhouse. I stared.

Shane waited for me to finish my sentence. When I didn't, he looked in the direction I was looking and gasped.

"KARLIN KILBURN! Absolutely not!" he scolded.

I startled, blinked, and looked at him.

"There's already a hole there…" I said slowly, as if in a trance. "…No one would ever know." My voice trailed off into a whisper.

I grinned, slightly maniacally.

Shane was horrified. He shook his head to make the words come out.

"Honey? … That's messed up!" he said, looking very concerned that his wife had such an idea.

"I know it is!" I laughed. "And of course I wouldn't!"

Shane was relieved, and we both laughed for several minutes. The look on his face was priceless—I wish I had recorded his reaction.

"Could you imagine, though?" I said, giggling. "Dumping her ashes in the outhouse would be absolutely—"

I was going to say *horrible*, but I lowered my voice in a serious tone and said, "—retribution."

Shane stopped laughing instantly. There was that concerned look again.

"Honey! … I'm just kidding!" I reassured him as I laughed so obnoxiously hard.

Shane faked a chuckle.

Again, I wish I had recorded him.

Back at home, Shane and I went to the laundry room and opened the cabinet.

Three boxes sat on the shelf, labeled Linda Rogers, R.K. Rogers, and James L. Davis—ashes of Shane's maternal grandparents and Daddy's.

Shane placed Sandy next to Daddy.

I looked at the shelf in somber thought and reverence.

"How did we end up being the crypt keepers?" I mumbled.

CHAPTER 19
Trifecta

As I replay all these childhood memories, one theme keeps recurring. We were not cherished.

We were not cherished by key people who, simply by their positions, could have made lasting, meaningful, positive differences in our lives.

As a mother and stepmother myself, I look back at the three young girls we were, and how uncherished we were by our parents… and I cry for them. But not for long. Because we're not there anymore.

They were flawed—Mom, Dad, and Sandy, as we all are. I pray to God my kids don't remember my sins during their tender formative years.

But, goodness gracious! Can we just agree that these three really did a number?!?

MOM

Mom was out of control!

Her control switch – for her temper, her emotions, her words, her reactions, her reasoning, EVERYTHING – was literally broken. Did she seek to have it repaired? I think not. Mom lived for herself; her children were inconveniently in her way. And when she was angry or couldn't have her way, she sought to cause physical pain and emotional hurt. The few times I recall seeing the slightest amount of remorse were when she drew blood.

She was mean.

Daddy was weak.

He could have been—and should have been—our protector, but he failed. Both times, he married strong-willed, self-serving women who emasculated him, and he couldn't stand up to them when it mattered. No matter how much I want to put Daddy on a pedestal, his passivity made him complicit in Sandy's cause.

Dad's little brother told me another story. Shortly before Daddy enlisted in the US Navy, he and a girlfriend were waiting at a bus stop when he was mugged at knifepoint. Daddy refused to give up his wallet. There was a struggle. And Daddy BIT OFF his attacker's FINGER!

Where was that backbone for his daughters?

Sandy was a troubled soul.

Something must have happened in her youth that made her desperate enough to hitchhike alone across the country and disappear from her family for the rest of her life. When I think about the phrase "hurt people, hurt people," I see Sandy. But I still don't excuse her.

When all hope for a relationship with Mom vanished, I had hoped for a better connection with Sandy. Yet after Daddy died and Sandy's bitterness heavily tainted everything, I still kept hoping. I guess I have an uncanny knack for always hoping for what might be possible. Kind of like the glass half full attitude? As long as we were both alive, why not hope, try, and keep hoping?

It's typical, expected, and even advised to cut ties with toxic people. I don't disagree. But I chose not to. Something in my spirit didn't feel right about that. Perhaps pitying her made it a little easier for me?

Sandy was broken.

***

... Remember those Survivor Benefits checks for my sisters and me that were mailed to my dad and Sandy?

After Daddy died, the checks continued coming to him for us from Mom's death, *and* Sandy started receiving them for us, from Daddy's death. So, who was depositing those checks sent to my dad? *Who* was endorsing them?? Not me or my sisters! We were minors. We didn't have bank accounts.

Just recently, as I was preparing for retirement, I looked up my Social Security information. At the top of the page, in bold red letters, it read "OVERPAYMENT."

I had been overpaid approximately $9800 in benefits.

I informed Ellen and Lulu, and they reported the same information.

Apparently, no one notified Social Security to stop sending the checks to my dad because he was now deceased. Also, Social Security didn't catch its own error for several years! – Minors are only allowed survivor benefits on one deceased parent at a time. At least that was the law back in the 70s and 80s.

So this is why Sandy was *asking* each of us for $10K. She *knew!*

Oh Sandy! Sandy, Sandy, Sandy! Even from the grave, you're still sticking it to us.

CHAPTER 20
Joan

In October 1943, Alice was 15 years old, living with her grandparents in the Philippines.

It was World War 2, and the Imperial Japanese Army (IJA) invaded Alice's village.

Several IJA soldiers raped Alice, and then they executed her grandparents in front of her.

Nine months later, Alice gave birth to a healthy baby girl, and the midwife who delivered her was Remegia Abing—*my* grandma Remy.

Alice told the midwife that she couldn't pay for her services, that she was only 15 and had no means or way to take care of a baby. So she asked Remy to take her baby and raise her.

Remy agreed. And she named the baby girl, Joan Elizabeth Abing.

Remy also promised Alice that she would notify her when Joan graduated from high school so that she could be part of the occasion.

Growing up with the Abings, Mom had a hard time being accepted by the rest of the extended family. It was mostly the adults who snubbed her, though. Her cousins saw no distinction.

Even after Auntie Suzette was born nearly 6 years later, people only referred to my mom as someone just part of the Abing family, not acknowledging that she was Remy's and Tito's daughter. And though Grandma Remy did a good job squashing such misgivings, clarifying that Joan was their daughter and she is to be respected as such, it still hurt Mom's heart. Auntie Suzette saw her sister's struggle with it.

When graduation came, Mom met her half-siblings, a sister and a brother. When she learned that her half-sister's name was Elizabeth, Mom was so moved.

"My middle name is Elizabeth!" my mom said with her hand over her heart, feeling a sense of connection.

NO RECORD

In 1965, Mom was 21 and working at her cousin's sari-sari store in Manila. A sari-sari store is a tiny sundry store unique to the Philippines. This is where my mom met Petty Officer Davis. James Luvern Davis—*my* dad.

When their relationship became serious, Mom told her parents about him: "This is the one." But, it didn't go very well…

First, he was an American. "Oh no! Oh no!"
Then he was in the military. "Oh no! Oh no! Oh no, noooo!"

But that all changed once they met him.

Mom told Grandma Remy that she needed her birth certificate to marry Dad. Grandma didn't have a copy, so she asked Alice if she had one.

"No manang, I don't have one," Alice told Grandma Remy. "I was only 15, and I didn't know what to do. That's why I gave her to you."

Mom's adoption was unofficial.

"You mean… if I die today… there is no record of me? As if I never existed?" She cried.

Mom's heart was so crushed; everyone cried with her.

It had been the bane of her existence in the Abing family—trying to be accepted, trying to fit in, trying to *be* someone. Now, she truly felt like she was no one.

However, there *is* a happy ending! They found a way to get my mom a birth certificate, and my parents got married!

Both Auntie Suzette and Mom's half-sister, Elizabeth, were in her wedding.

Then, in April 1966, I made my debut at the Naval Station at Sangley Point, Cavite City, Philippines.

In May 1967, Ellen was born at Travis Air Force Base in California.

And in August 1969, we were back in the Philippines when Lulu was born.

We came to the States permanently in 1972.

By 1974, Mom and Dad divorced.

In 1976, Dad remarried Sandy.

Between 1977 and 1978, Mom told Ellen she regretted divorcing Daddy.

In the summer of 1978, Daddy came over to visit Mom. I think he came to tell her that he was being stationed at NAS Meridian, Mississippi. – That's when I walked in on Mom sitting on Daddy's lap with her arms around his neck.

Then, roughly 6 months later, he attended her funeral. And cried.

This might be a stretch, but I'm going to connect the dots…

I believe Mom and Dad had a love story they could no longer pursue because of the choices they made, specifically that one of them had already remarried.

But what if their conversation, while Mom was on his lap, was about something hopeful for the future? However, her funeral made that impossible, and those were the tears Daddy cried.

And what if Sandy somehow knew? So she made me the scapegoat for all her jealousies.

CHAPTER 21
Who am I?

What are the odds that these three people in such vital positions would not fulfill their expected roles and responsibilities? What if that was part of God's plan?

What if they, by design, couldn't give my sisters and me what we needed? What if they were rendered incapable for a purpose? And, what if it was meant for me to keep hoping and pursuing?

Remember Exodus? God hardened Pharaoh's heart for His purpose. (Exodus 7 and 8).

I used to jokingly say, "I learned what *not* to do from my parents. Har har har!" Well, I'm not joking anymore. Subsequently, I learned what *to* do as well.

Yes, it was harrowing. Yes, I questioned if the pain was necessary to learn what God wanted me to understand. But since He created me, knitted me together in Mom's womb, God inarguably knows me better than I know myself. Right? If I even dared to ask Him about it, I think our conversation would sound similar to the one He had with Job (Job 38-41).

So, at nearly 60 years old, I can confidently say that the pain has shaped me.

Mom was reactive and deceitful. Dad was (oh, I hate to say this, but)... a coward. And Sandy was intentional.

Every spiteful action Sandy took was thoughtfully planned. "How can I bully Karlin today because she looks like her dead mother?" and "What can I do so I don't have to look at her face every day?"

Then I think of Joseph and how he ended up in Egypt.

You intended to harm me, but God intended it for good *to accomplish what is now being done, the saving of many lives. – Genesis 50:20*

And Isaiah 54:17:
*"...**no weapon forged against you will prevail,** and you will refute every tongue that accuses you. This is the heritage of the servants of the LORD, and this is their vindication from me," declares the LORD.*

The *good* was French Camp Academy, the Egypt I thrived in. With it, Sandy sought to cause hurt by separating me from my sisters. She wanted to rid her daily life of the reminder that her husband had a life before her. That was her weapon.

During my Egypt, I was growing in stature and wisdom in the Lord. Everything I learned molded me into who I am today. Every verse memorized was hidden in my heart so I would not sin against the Lord (Psalm 119:11).

***

However, I would be remiss not to mention my backslide.

I backslid so badly and so far that I surpassed my mom's lifestyle, which I had been so critical of. If it were a contest, I would have won. Mom probably rolled over in her grave, exclaiming, "Ay, Anak! I didn't even do that!" – Sandy calling me a whore in my teens came to fruition.

Train up a child in the way he should go: and when he is old, he will not depart from it. – Proverbs 22:6

FCA trained me up in that way, and I didn't depart from it, per se. But I did sweep it under the rug for over a decade. This was my Egypt of sin and bondage.

But praise God for all the seeds that had been planted intentionally *and* accidentally! He used my sons to U-turn me back to Him, making me a prodigal daughter. –

With all that I am, Father, thank You for Your compassion and grace. You were so incredibly patient with me - slow to anger - You gave me mercies I don't deserve. I'm so sorry you saw the things I've done. I accept and receive Your forgiveness, Lord. Please help me to forgive myself.

You are worthy, Lord. You alone are worthy of my next breath, my next heartbeat. And I will worship You and sing of Your goodness forever.

***

Matthew 5:44-45:

"But I tell you, **love your enemies and pray for those who persecute you,** *that you may be sons of your Father in heaven. He causes His sun to rise on the evil and the good, and sends rain on the righteous and the unrighteous."*

Who can love their attacker while getting beaten up, raped, held at gunpoint and shot, stabbed, strangled, drowned … beheaded? … whipped 39 lashes, then nailed to a cross?

Loving Sandy while she was beating me with that stick never crossed my mind. But I thought about it on that Christmas Day in 2023.

I thought about what I *didn't* do for a poor widow in my family. I've tried easing my conscience, reminding myself that Sandy was a recluse, a hermit. That was how she wanted to live. Heck, she was probably ok with dying the way she did! But what I couldn't shake off was that I didn't visit more often, to offer her my assistance, or … just my friendship.

In short, I didn't do enough! And in hindsight, I'd rather she rejected all my offers than have to stand before God and explain why I barely offered anything at all. That I was lazy, that I was too cozy in my comfort zone. *I'm sorry, Jesus.*

I have been given much grace. Jesus has forgiven me of my sins. Who am I to hold a grudge and withhold either? No one. I am no one special. Even though I was the one who was hurt.

My life was difficult for me. But others have suffered far worse, unthinkable tragedies that make mine look like a cake walk. So again, who am I to hold a grudge? I am *absolutely* no one!

I've refused to let my life's pain serve as a crutch, blaming my bad decisions on the past (and I definitely made some doozies). I own all my mistakes. No matter who influenced me, past or present, I take responsibility for every bad decision I've ever made.

I've refused to see myself as a victim of my past. Yes, I *was* a victim, but I am no longer a victim.

I still refuse because God placed me in those specific environments with those particular people for a purpose, for a season. I know that sounds overused, cliché, and boring.

But if God gives you the opportunity – and I pray He does! – to reflect on your past, to see all the mountains and valleys you've crossed so far; to recognize when He walked right beside you, carried you, or, as He's done with me many times, dragged you along; to acknowledge all His provisions… and those you've rejected; to realize when He and the Heavenly Host cheered for you and rejoiced… and when God collected all your tears in His bottle, you'd be overwhelmed! Mind blown! In complete awe!

You'd lift your hands and sing hallelujah at the top of your lungs, then fall to your knees sobbing, "But why me, Lord? Why do You love me so much to be so patient with me?" Then you'll realize that holding grudges, withholding forgiveness, blaming others for your decisions, and staying a victim (in your mind) are contrary to what the Creator teaches.

…Sorry. I got a little preachy there.

In my youth, I didn't know how to ask God for deliverance from my Egypts. But He delivered me from two of them – Mom and Sandy – without my asking, and He made me flourish in another (FCA), all in His perfect time.

In every phase of my life, God was faithfully with me. Though I left Him for a season and He witnessed all my debaucheries, He was never out of reach.

He's even given in to a few of my temper tantrums, letting me have my own way, only to come to my rescue *again*, picking up my shattered pieces, and whispering to me, "I told you this was not good." His tender mercies are so humbling. I surely don't deserve them. Yet, this is how He loves.

And finally, what does forgiveness really look like, especially when Jesus tells us to forgive our offenders seventy times seven (Matthew 18:21-22)?

I know what it *doesn't* look like. – It doesn't look like cutting ties or loving them from a safe distance, so they can't hurt us again.

It sounds like we're actually living close enough that they'll hurt us again, over and over —seventy times seven. It's messy. It hurts. But how else could we practice Colossians 3:13 if we cut them off?

Bear with each other *and forgive one another if any of you has a grievance against someone.* ***Forgive as the Lord forgave you.***

This is why I didn't cut ties with Sandy. I *need* God's forgiveness.

So now, when I ask, Who am I? The answer is:

I am His...

Who am I, that the Lord of all the earth
Would care to know my name
Would care to feel my hurt?
Who am I, that the Bright and Morning Star
Would choose to light the way
For my ever wandering heart?

Not because of who I am
But because of what You've done
Not because of what I've done
But because of who You are

I am a flower quickly fading
Here today and gone tomorrow
A wave tossed in the ocean
A vapor in the wind
Still, You hear me when I'm calling
Lord, You catch me when I'm falling
And You've told me who I am
I am Yours, I am Yours

Who am I, that the eyes that see my sin
Would look on me with love and watch me rise again?
Who am I, that the voice that calmed the sea
Would call out through the rain
And calm the storm in me?

Not because of who I am
But because of what You've done
Not because of what I've done
But because of who You are
I am a flower quickly fading
Here today and gone tomorrow
A wave tossed in the ocean
A vapor in the wind
Still, You hear me when I'm calling
Lord, You catch me when I'm falling
And You've told me who I am
I am Yours

– *"Who am I" by Casting Crowns, 2003*

CHAPTER 22
Letters

Hope is why I stood on Sandy's front porch, knocking on her door that she would never open again. Things didn't end the way I had imagined, but I am very much at peace knowing that I never gave up hope. Of the three things that remain, hope is one of them (1 Corinthians 13:13).

If the Lord said, "Karlin, you can write a letter to each of them right now, I'll make sure they read it," I'd write …

Dear Mom,

I visited Auntie Suzette a couple of months ago and introduced her to Shane. She thinks you would highly approve of him as well. She also told me stories about you and her, and though I've always loved you, I fell in love with you again.

I have spent most of my life trying to understand you. I've replayed memories over and over, wondering what I did wrong, why you were so hard on me, why it always felt like I was the one you didn't want.

I was so young. I needed you to like me. Not just love me, but *really* like me. And I don't think you did. That hurt in a way I didn't have words for back then. So I carried it. For years.

But I also remember other things. I remember your perfume, your music, the way your presence filled a room; your smile, your laugh. Our last night together as two young women getting ready for dates. – If only time could stand still, I'd stay in that moment a little longer with you. You worked hard, provided for us, and gave us life. And somehow, even through everything, I never stopped loving you.

When you died, everything froze. I didn't get to ask you questions. I didn't get to grow up and understand you as a woman, not just as my mother. I was left with pieces. And I've spent a lifetime trying to put them together.

I don't excuse what you did. But I see you differently now. I see a woman who wrestled with her own past. A woman who was searching for something she would never find. A woman who didn't know how to love without pain attached to it. A woman who gave what she had, even if it wasn't what we needed.

I wish things had been different. I wish you had liked me. I wish I could have known what it felt like to be safe with you. But I don't live in that wish anymore.

I forgive you, Mamma.

Not because it didn't matter, but because it *did.*

You know, when I do my makeup and fix my hair, sometimes I see you… and it comforts me. It's like a part of you has been with me all along.

I miss you. I wish I had more time with you, and I have so much more to tell you! If you never knew then, I hope you can know now that I love you. I've always loved you.

Your Ugly Duckling,
Karlin

Dear Dad,

Daddy, I want you to know that my husband, Shane, is everything you would have wanted in a husband for me, who I could be that good wife for. He is the man you could have entrusted your princess to had you had the opportunity.

I birthed four boys, Daddy. I sure wish they could have known you and learned about the great outdoors from you, as I did. – I did teach Scott how to fish and clean them, though. Just like you taught me. – Scott looks the most like you, Daddy.

When I was 30, I enlisted in the US Navy Reserves! Remember when I was 7 and I said I wanted to be in the Navy just like you? And you said, "Oh no, Peanut! The Navy is no place for a lady!" Obviously, I didn't take you seriously, or it flew right over my head. Either way, I had hoped to influence my boys' military duty when I noticed their priorities for a college education didn't match mine (or yours). And it worked! Two enlisted in the Air Force and one in the Army.

My Army son, Kellen, was a medic and sustained an IED explosion while in Afghanistan in 2012. After years of recovery and therapy, he is doing very well. He keeps a beard to hide his scars, but a blackout contact lens for his right eye reminds us all of his TBI residuals. But God is good! – He has your green eyes.

Daddy, you were my safe place. In a world that didn't always feel safe, you were gentle. You were kind. I will never forget the way you showed up for me, bringing me what I needed at school. Calling me "Peanut." Teaching me things most girls didn't learn. You made me feel seen. And loved.

But there were times I needed more from you. I needed you to stand up. To protect us. To say, "This isn't okay." And you didn't.

I didn't understand it then. And for a long time, I didn't understand it as an adult either. But I see you more clearly now. You were a gentle man in hard situations. And sometimes gentleness looks like silence. Even when it shouldn't.

You loved us the best way you knew how. And I never doubted that. Not once. I just wish your love had been louder. Stronger. More protective. But even with that, you were still, and will always be, my hero. And part of me will always be that little girl so in awe of her daddy. –I forgive you.

And I thank you. I thank you for everything you gave us, and even for what you couldn't.

I miss you so much, Daddy.

Your one and only,
Peanut

Dear Sandy,

I wasn't going to write this. Not because I don't have anything to say, but because I have too much. Then I realized I had to…

You came into my life at a time when I needed a mother, a friend, or just someone supportive. And I wanted to believe you could be that for my sisters and me. I really did.

But instead, we hurt each other. Over and over again. You said things that stayed with me. You made me feel small. Unwanted. Like, there was something wrong with me.

And I know I didn't make it easy either. I talked back. I pushed back. I fought you. Because I didn't understand why you were so against us. Especially me.

Now I think… maybe you didn't understand either. You wanted something that was never really yours. A child. A connection. A place in a family that already existed before you. And I think I reminded you of that.

We were both standing in the same house, feeling like we didn't belong.

I came back for you. You know that, right? After all those years, I came back. I wanted to rebuild something with you. I wanted something different for us.

But I was too late.

And for a while, that sat heavy on me. Until I realized something. Maybe forgiveness doesn't need a moment. Maybe it doesn't need a conversation. Maybe it just needs a decision. So here it is…

I forgive you.

I forgive you for the things you said. For the way you treated me. For the hurt we never fully resolved, but just swept under the rug.

And I forgive myself for the resentment I carried. For the grace I didn't always give you. For the expectation I had of you, to give us something you couldn't, to be someone you weren't.

We were both broken in different ways. And now… I let it go.

I hope you found peace. And I hope—somewhere, somehow—you know that I tried.

Goodbye, Sandy.

"For I know the plans I have for you," declares the Lord,
"plans to prosper you and not to harm you,
plans to give you hope and a future."

Jeremiah 29:11

Dear Reader,

There is no predicament that God can't see you through or rescue you from. All you have to do is call out to Him, just like a 9-year-old girl did.

When you pass through the waters, I will be with you; and when
you pass through the rivers, they will not sweep over you.
When you walk through the fire, you will not be burned;
the flames will not set you ablaze.

Isaiah 43:2

Father God,
I pray the reader of this book will come to know Your love and faithfulness, as I have. Lord, let them feel Your hand unmistakably in their life. Call them, Father, and help them come to You, for their eternal benefit, and for Your ultimate glory. That goodness and mercy shall follow them all the days of their life as they dwell in Your house forever. – There is no one like You, Lord.

In Jesus Name, Amen.

Karlin